DODECANESE

TRAVEL GUIDE 2025

Unlock the Magic of Rhodes, Kos, Patmos &
Symi with Insider Paths, Hidden Beaches &
Authentic Encounters

Mary D. Smith

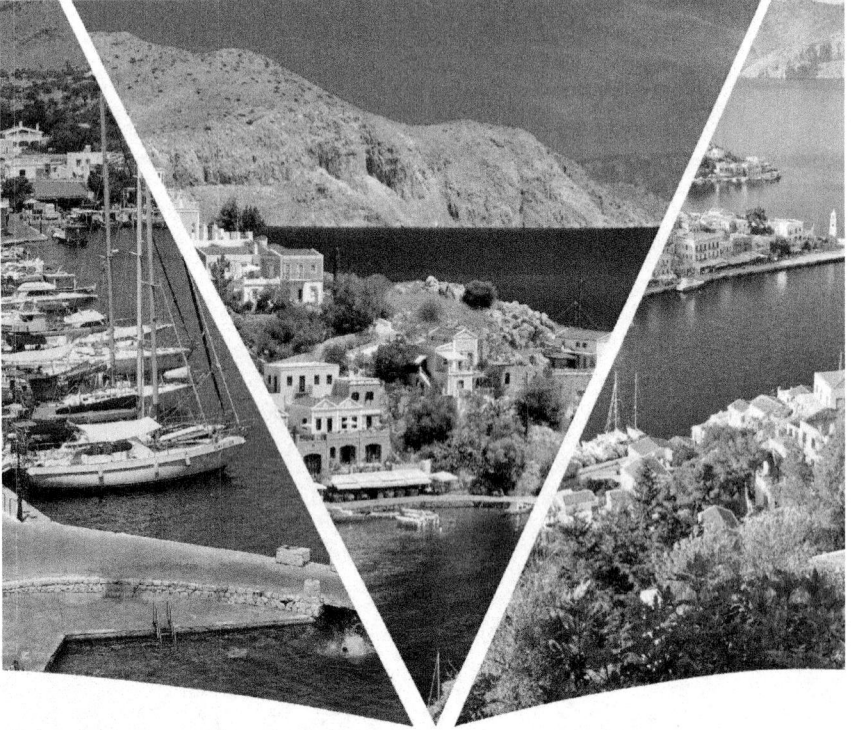

Welcome

To

Dodecanese

Disclaimer

The world is constantly changing, hotels change ownership or close, restaurants might adjust their prices, museum could alter their closing hours, and transportation routes can be modified.

This changes can happen even after our author have visited, inspected and written about these places

While we strive to keep all information as current as possible, some changes may inevitable occur before a new edition of this guidebook is published.

Thanks you for choosing our guidebook, we hope you have an amazing trip

About the Author

Mary D. Smith is a travel writer, explorer, and storyteller with an eye for the hidden corners of the world—and a deep love for the soul of the Mediterranean. For over a decade, she has wandered off the beaten path to uncover places that don't just look beautiful, but feel meaningful. Her writing blends practical guidance with a personal touch, offering readers more than just itineraries—it offers perspective, emotion, and connection.

Her fascination with the Dodecanese began with a spontaneous trip to Patmos that turned into a month-long odyssey through whitewashed villages, volcanic craters, forgotten monasteries, and meals shared with locals who welcomed her like family. That journey sparked a commitment: to create a guide that honours the spirit of these islands and helps others experience them with the same depth and joy.

Mary believes in slow travel, getting lost on purpose, and saying yes to the unexpected. Through her work, she encourages others to look beyond the obvious and find the stories that make travel unforgettable.

This guide is a reflection of her journey—and an invitation to begin yours.

A Heartfelt Thank You

To every traveller who's ever wandered down an unmarked path, taken the wrong ferry, or stayed just a little longer because the sunset was too beautiful to leave—this book was written with you in mind.

Thank you for trusting me to be part of your journey through the Dodecanese. Creating this guide has been more than research—it's been a labour of love, fuelled by conversations with locals, shared meals in quiet courtyards, and moments of awe in ancient chapels and hidden bays.

To the kind strangers who offered directions, stories, and smiles along the way—your generosity shaped this guide more than you know. And to you, the reader: thank you for choosing this book. I hope it brings you joy, insight, and a sense of wonder.

May your journey be filled with meaning, and may the Dodecanese stay with you long after you've left its shores.

Table of Contents

Dodecanese

Scan The QR Code

1. Open your phone's camera.

2. Point it at the QR code.

3. Wait for a link to appear.

4. Tap the link.

5. Follow the instructions on-screen.

CHAPTER

1

The Dodecanese at a Glance

Welcome to the Dodecanese

The Dodecanese islands are where time slows down and mythology breathes through sun-drenched stones, whitewashed villages, and cobalt waters that seem painted by the gods. Set like a shimmering necklace in the south eastern Aegean Sea, this island chain of twelve main islands—and dozens of islets—feels like a different Greece altogether: wilder in parts, polished in others, but always authentic, always rewarding.

Each island tells a different story. Rhodes dazzles with its medieval Old Town and cosmopolitan flair. Symi glows like a pastel jewel with its neoclassical harbor. Patmos whispers sacred secrets, while Kalymnos calls rock climbers from across the globe. Some islands, like Kos and Karpathos, balance beach life with ancient ruins and mountain villages. Others, like Tilos and Nisyros, quietly surprise you with eco-conscious charm or volcanic drama.

This guide will take you beyond the tourist trail and into the hidden courtyards, forgotten paths, and sunset moments that make the Dodecanese more than a destination—it's a feeling. Whether you're here for two days or two months, the Dodecanese offers more than just places to see. It offers stories to live.

And here's the truth: once you've visited one island, you'll want to visit them all. Because island-hopping here isn't just convenient—it's addictive.

Who This Guide is for (First-Timers, Families, Adventurers, Culture Seekers)

Whether you're booking your first Greek island holiday or returning for your fifth, this guide is crafted to meet you where you are—and take you further than you expected.

For First-Timers:

If you've never been to the Dodecanese—or even to Greece—this guide offers a well-paced, clearly explained roadmap. You'll learn how to choose the right island for your personality, when to go, how to get around, and what to avoid. There's no jargon, no assumptions. We guide you through the maze of ferries, festivals, and foreign menus with clarity and confidence.

For Families:

Planning a family getaway? We've got you covered with recommendations for kid-friendly beaches, family-run tavernas, and calm islands with safe, shallow waters. We also point out where strollers won't work and where adventurous teens will thrive. From castle-hopping in Rhodes to donkey spotting in Hydra (yes, really), this guide makes family travel smoother and more enriching.

For Adventurers:

Love to hike, dive, sail, or climb? The Dodecanese is your playground. This guide gives you the inside track on climbing cliffs in Kalymnos, hiking ancient trails in Karpathos, diving into volcanic craters off Nisyros, or kayaking from cove to cove in remote Lipsi. You won't just find activities—you'll find epic routes, gear rental tips, and local contacts.

For Culture Seekers & History Buffs:

If your suitcase has more books than swimsuits, you'll love what's ahead. This guide goes deep into the rich layers of the Dodecanese: from Byzantine monasteries and Ottoman architecture to Crusader castles and sacred caves. Whether you're tracing the steps of St. John in Patmos or hunting mosaics in Kos, we help you uncover context, not just landmarks.

For Solo Travelers, Couples, Digital Nomads, and Slow Travelers:

Looking for solitude, romance, or a long-term escape? We've included tips on remote stays, co-working-friendly cafes, and soulful moments—because the Dodecanese can feel like a private retreat or an open invitation, depending on how you travel.

Bottom line: whoever you are, there's a version of the Dodecanese waiting for you. And this guide helps you meet it.

What's New in 2025: Events, Routes & Updates

Even places steeped in history evolve—and the Dodecanese in 2025 is as dynamic as it is ancient. Whether you're returning or arriving for the first time, here's what's new this year:

Expanded Ferry Services & Faster Connections:

The Greek Ministry of Maritime Affairs has introduced a new high-speed ferry route linking Rhodes–Symi–Kos–Patmos–Leros with reduced travel time. This is a game-changer for travelers aiming to visit multiple islands without losing precious daylight.

Eco-Friendly Initiatives & Green Travel:

Several islands—most notably Tilos and Astypalaia—have ramped up sustainability efforts. Expect new electric shuttle services, solar-powered accommodations, and locally run eco-experiences. Tilos, already known for its zero-waste goal, now offers guided eco-walks that explore its biodiversity and rewilding projects.

New Hiking Trails & Outdoor Adventures:

Karpathos and Kalymnos have introduced well-marked trail networks with English signage and updated GPS mapping apps for hikers and bikers. In Nisyros, volcanic crater walks now include immersive audio guides developed by local students, bringing ancient geology to life.

Cultural Events & Festival Updates:

Rhodes hosts the inaugural "Aegean Light Festival" in late June 2025, celebrating island music, storytelling, and food with artists from across the Mediterranean. Patmos has expanded its Sacred Music Festival to include contemporary spiritual performances, drawing global talent and new audiences.

Digital Nomad Infrastructure:

Kos and Rhodes are becoming hotspots for long-stay travelers, with new co-working hubs, fiber-optic internet in popular areas, and incentives for digital nomads staying over 30 days. If you're mixing business with Aegean views, the Dodecanese is now a serious contender.

Cultural Preservation Projects:

Several restoration efforts are underway, including the medieval fortifications of Rhodes and the Monastery of Saint John in Patmos. These projects mean travelers in 2025 can witness the region's heritage not only as static ruins but as living history being preserved.

Flight and Access Updates:

Kos and Rhodes have added new seasonal international routes from Northern and Eastern Europe. SkyExpress has also introduced a new domestic air pass for multi-island travelers—worth considering if time is short but your wish list is long.

Now is an ideal time to explore the Dodecanese. The islands are doubling down on what makes them special—while making it easier, greener, and more immersive to experience them.

How to Use This Guide (Navigation Tips, Symbols, Icons)

This isn't just a book to flip through. This is your Dodecanese travel toolkit, inspiration board, and navigation companion. It's been designed with both planners and spontaneous wanderers in mind. Whether you're on a beach lounger in Kos, boarding a ferry in Rhodes, or mapping your entire Greek summer from your couch in Copenhagen, this guide fits into your journey—wherever you are in it.

Start Broad, Then Zoom In

Begin with the island overviews in this first section. If you're still deciding *where* to go, that's your map. Once you've chosen your islands, head to their dedicated chapters—each one is structured like a mini guidebook, complete with local secrets and handpicked highlights.

Use the Sections Like Chapters in a Story

This guide flows from big-picture planning to on-the-ground discovery. Think of it as a journey:

- The beginning helps you choose the right islands
- The middle dives into getting there, moving around, and finding the best experiences
- The end includes cultural tips, insider insights, food highlights, and a bonus journal section to personalize your adventure

You don't have to read everything in order—but everything is there for a reason.

Action Tips, Local Secrets, Must-Knows

Throughout the guide, you'll see special formatting to help you scan quickly when you're on the go. No confusing symbols or overdone icons—just clear cues that tell you what matters:

- **Local Tip:** Straight from a resident or seasoned traveller—things you wouldn't find on a tourist brochure.
- **Quick Insight:** Need-to-know info, whether it's ferry logistics or dress codes for monasteries.
- **Worth the Detour:** Slightly off-path recommendations that are well worth your time.

- **Avoid This Trap:** Honest advice about what might not be worth the hype or how to avoid common mistakes.

Travel Styles Included

Whether you're traveling luxuriously, minimally, solo, with kids, or as a couple, this guide calls out when a place is especially good (or tricky) for that style of traveller.

Quick Island Overview: Snapshot Comparisons

The Dodecanese includes 12 main islands and over 150 smaller ones—don't worry, you don't need to visit them all (unless you're planning an odyssey). Here's a quick-reference snapshot to help you see the big picture.

Dodecanese Island Comparison Chart

Island	Vibe	Best For	Known For	How Long to Stay	Skip If
Rhodes	Cosmopolitan, Historic	First-timers, Culture lovers, Nightlife	Medieval Old Town, Beaches, Castles	3–5 days	You want secluded quiet
Kos	Lively, Accessible	Families, Beach lovers, Cyclists	Roman ruins, Sandy beaches	2–4 days	You want dramatic terrain

Island	Vibe	Best For	Known For	How Long to Stay	Skip If
Symi	Charming, Elegant	Romantic getaways, Photographers	Colorful harbor, Day trips	1–2 days	You need a beach vacation
Patmos	Spiritual, Serene	History buffs, Pilgrims, Writers	Monastery of St. John, Sacred Cave	2–3 days	You're after nightlife
Kalymnos	Rugged, Adventurous	Climbers, Divers, Hikers	World-class climbing, Sponge diving	2–4 days	You need luxury services
Karpathos	Wild, Authentic	Hikers, Culture seekers, Road trippers	Mountain villages, Traditions	3–5 days	You're short on time
Leros	Low-key, Local	Slow travelers, Repeat visitors	Italian architecture, Hidden beaches	1–3 days	You want vibrant nightlife
Tilos	Quiet, Green	Eco-travelers	Rewilding project, Nature hikes	1–2 days	You want built-up tourism

Island	Vibe	Best For	Known For	How Long to Stay	Skip If
Nisyros	Dramatic, Underrated	Volcano lovers, Photographers	Live volcanic crater, Thermal baths	1–2 days	You have mobility issues
Astypalaia	Chic, Remote	Couples, Explorers	Butterfly-shaped island, Boutique vibe	2–4 days	You want easy access
Lipsi	Tiny, Peaceful	Solo travelers, Writers, Yogis	Simplicity, Friendly locals	1–2 days	You need high energy
Kastellorizo	Remote, Magical	Off-the-grid dreamers	Blue Cave, Turkish border views	1 day	You dislike ferry transfers

A full-color fold-out-style map is included at the beginning of the print guide and hyperlinked in the digital version. This visual breakdown helps you understand island clusters, ferry routes, and proximity.

Choosing the Right Islands for Your Trip

Let's make one thing clear: there's no such thing as the *best* Dodecanese island—only the best one(s) for you. Your time, travel style, and interests will determine what's perfect. This guide helps you match your needs to the right destination.

If You're a First-Time Visitor to Greece:

Start with Rhodes or Kos. They're easy to access by air and ferry, packed with a variety of experiences, and well set up for tourists without feeling overdone. From ancient sites to nightlife, from shopping to beaches, they let you sample it all.

If You Crave Peace, Simplicity, and Authenticity:

Try Tilos, Lipsi, or Leros. These smaller islands are where time slows. They're ideal if you want to journal, hike, disconnect, or enjoy meals where the chef and server are the same person. No loud scooters. No beach clubs. Just pure atmosphere.

If You're into Adventure and the Outdoors:

Kalymnos, Karpathos, and Nisyros will be your playground. Climbing, hiking, biking, and diving are more than activities— they're part of the island culture. You'll find challenging terrain and unforgettable views.

If Culture, History, and Sacred Sites Call to You:

Patmos is a must for spiritual seekers and history lovers. For those interested in ancient medicine, ruins, and healing, Kos offers a Hippocratic journey. Rhodes and Karpathos offer a deep dive into medieval and traditional cultures.

If You're Traveling with Family:

Kos is the most family-friendly thanks to sandy beaches and flat terrain. Rhodes also works well, especially the southern coast. Avoid the remote or mountainous islands unless your kids are up for rustic adventures.

If You're Romancing or Honeymooning:

Symi, Astypalaia, and Lipsi offer postcard-worthy views and intimate vibes. Quiet harbors, candlelit tavernas, and scenic walks make these ideal for couples.

If You Want to See Multiple Islands:

Plan a cluster trip. Example:

- Rhodes – Symi – Tilos (history, charm, nature)
- Kos – Nisyros – Kalymnos (culture, volcano, adventure)
- Patmos – Leros – Lipsi (sacred, hidden, soulful)

Each cluster is designed for ferry-friendly travel without constant packing and unpacking.

Tip: Don't Try to Do It All

The Dodecanese rewards depth, not just distance. It's better to experience 2–3 islands well than skim through 6 and forget the names. Choose your rhythm, follow your curiosity, and let the Aegean work its magic.

CHAPTER

2

Essential Trip Planning

Best Time to Visit & Seasonal Insights

A sk a local when the best time to visit the Dodecanese is, and you'll get a knowing smile. The truth is, every season offers something magical, depending on what kind of traveller you are. Whether you're chasing sunsets on a quiet beach or dancing at a summer festival, the Dodecanese reveals different personalities throughout the year.

Spring (March to May): Quiet Beauty & Authenticity

If you're a traveller who seeks genuine connection, fresh air, and quiet cobbled streets, spring is your season. Wildflowers explode across the countryside—especially on Karpathos and Tilos. Villages awaken from their winter slumber, locals repaint tavernas, and Orthodox Easter brings some of the most authentic, community-driven celebrations you'll ever experience.

Pros:

- Ideal weather for hiking and exploring historical sites
- Fewer tourists = better prices and deeper conversations
- Wildflowers and green landscapes
- Orthodox Easter: culturally rich but avoid ferry congestion during peak days

Cons:

- Some tourist services may still be limited in early March
- Sea temperature is still cool for swimming

Summer (June to August): Vibrant, Warm, and Alive

This is peak season—when the ferries are full, the tavernas are buzzing, and beach life is in full swing. July and August bring long, hot days and lively nights, particularly on Rhodes, Kos, and Symi, where you'll find open-air cinemas, waterfront bars, and plenty of summer festivals.

Pros:

- Full range of tours, ferries, and excursions
- Excellent nightlife and beach scenes
- Lots of cultural festivals (especially in August)

Cons:

- Crowds in popular spots
- Higher prices for accommodation
- Intense heat, especially midday

Tip: Visit in late June or early September for that sweet spot between full-swing summer and peaceful exploration.

Autumn (September to October): Golden Light & Local Charm

Autumn is when the Aegean exhales. The sea is still warm, crowds start to thin, and locals have time to relax and chat again. This is harvest season, too—grapes, figs, and olives—and you can feel the land's generosity everywhere you go.

Pros:

- Still-swimmable waters
- Shoulder-season pricing
- A quieter, more authentic rhythm

Cons:

- Some ferry routes and tours may reduce frequency mid-October onward
- Shorter days as the season progresses

Winter (November to February): Slow, Solitary, and Local

Not for everyone, but if you love stormy coastlines, uncrowded monasteries, and slow fireside meals, this might be your secret season. Patmos and Kalymnos keep a slower but steady winter community. Expect ferries to be weather-dependent and many hotels to be closed, but off-season travel offers unmatched intimacy.

Pros:

- Zero tourist crowds
- Best time for writers, researchers, and cultural immersion
- Significantly reduced prices

Cons:

- Limited flights and ferry services
- Some islands almost entirely shut down to visitors
- Cold, wet weather, especially in January

Final Verdict:

- June and September offer the best balance of beauty, access, and ease.
- Spring (April–May) is perfect for authenticity and hikes.
- Avoid August if you dislike crowds and heat, but embrace it if you want peak energy.
- Winter is best for long stays, spiritual retreats, or reconnecting with the rhythm of real island life.

Entry Requirements, Visas & Travel Regulations

Before you pack your sunscreen and sandals, you'll want to ensure your travel documents are in order. Thankfully, Greece is part of the Schengen Area, which makes things fairly straightforward—but there are nuances.

Visa & Entry Overview

Citizens of the EU/EEA/Switzerland:

- Can enter Greece with just a national ID card or passport.
- No visa required. No time limits on stay.

Citizens of the USA, UK, Canada, Australia, New Zealand, Japan, and many others:

- No visa required for stays under 90 days within any 180-day period.
- Must have a passport valid for at least 3 months beyond your departure.
- Starting late 2025, travelers will need ETIAS authorization (European Travel Information and Authorization System). This will be a simple online pre-approval, not a visa.

Tip: ETIAS is not yet live as of early 2025, but expected later in the year. Check the official EU ETIAS website before travel.

Other Nationals:

- May require a Schengen visa. Check with the Greek consulate or embassy in your country. Apply well in advance.

Entry Points to the Dodecanese

You can enter the Dodecanese either:

- By international flight: Airports in Rhodes and Kos serve seasonal and direct international flights.
- Via Athens: Fly into Athens and connect with a local flight or ferry.
- Via Turkey: Some travelers enter via ferries from Bodrum or Marmaris into Kos or Rhodes. A passport is required, and visa rules may differ depending on your nationality.

Health, Safety & Emergency Preparedness

Even the most carefree island dream needs a bit of smart planning. The Dodecanese is generally very safe, but preparation ensures you stay healthy, protected, and confident throughout your trip.

Healthcare in the Dodecanese

- Public Hospitals: Rhodes and Kos have fully functioning hospitals with emergency services. Other islands have smaller clinics or health centers.
- Pharmacies: Readily available even on small islands. Pharmacists are knowledgeable and often speak English.

- Private Care: On larger islands, you can access private doctors and labs with reasonable costs.

Tip: Bring any necessary prescriptions with a translated note if possible. Pharmacies can often help with minor ailments.

Health Insurance & Travel Coverage

It is strongly recommended to have travel insurance that covers:

- Emergency medical care
- Hospitalization
- Medical evacuation (especially important on remote islands)
- Trip cancellation/interruption

EU citizens should carry a European Health Insurance Card (EHIC) or its replacement, the EHIC Global (GHIC) if from the UK.

Emergency Numbers & Local Help

- 112 – Europe-wide emergency number (works for fire, police, ambulance)
- 166 – Greek emergency ambulance service
- 199 – Fire service
- 100 – Police

In case of minor issues, local tourism offices can help contact doctors, interpreters, or pharmacies.

Safety Tips

- Crime is low in the Dodecanese, especially on the smaller islands.
- Pickpocketing is rare but stay aware in busy markets, ports, and buses.

- Water is safe to drink in most towns but bottled water is preferred in remote areas.
- If hiking, bring proper gear and let someone know your route. Some paths are unmarked or exposed to heat.
- If renting scooters or ATVs, make sure your insurance covers it, and always wear a helmet.

Natural Hazards

- Heatwaves: Common in July–August. Stay hydrated, wear sun protection, and avoid peak sun hours.
- Wildfires: Rare but possible in dry months. Respect fire bans and report smoke.
- Earthquakes: Occasionally felt but rarely damaging. If one occurs, move away from buildings and stay calm.

Budget Planning: Costs, Currencies & Saving Tips

If you're wondering whether the Dodecanese is a budget-friendly paradise or a lavish Aegean escape, the answer is: it's both— depending on how you travel. You can sip €2 espresso in a village café or book a €600-a-night cliffside villa with infinity views. This region caters to backpackers, honeymooners, and everyone in between.

Understanding the Basics: Currency & Payment

- Currency: Euro (€)
- Cash vs. Card: Credit and debit cards are widely accepted, especially on larger islands like Rhodes, Kos, and Patmos. But smaller islands, village tavernas, and bus services may still prefer cash.

- ATMs: Easy to find in main towns but limited in remote areas. Always carry some cash, especially for island-hopping, ferries, or rural explorations.

Tip: Avoid airport currency exchange booths. Instead, withdraw Euros from ATMs using a debit card for better rates. Opt for machines from reputable banks like Alpha Bank or National Bank of Greece.

Average Daily Budget (Per Person)

Here's a breakdown of what you might expect to spend, depending on your travel style:

Type of Traveller	Daily Budget	Includes
Budget Traveller	€45–€70	Hostel/guesthouse, street food, public transport, free activities
Mid-Range	€90–€150	Boutique hotel, taverna meals, scooter rental, some paid tours
Luxury	€200+	High-end hotels, fine dining, private tours, ferry upgrades

Key Cost Areas

1. Accommodation:

- Dorm beds or basic rooms start at €25–€40 per night.
- Mid-range hotels range between €60–€120.
- Luxury resorts and villas can go €200–€600+, especially in peak season on Rhodes or Symi.

2. Food & Drink:

- Gyros or souvlaki wraps: €3–€5
- Taverna meal with house wine: €12–€20
- Seafood dinner for two with wine: €40–€70
- Espresso: €1.50–€3, Cocktail: €7–€12

3. Transportation:

- Inter-island ferry: €10–€40, depending on distance
- Local bus: €1.50–€3
- Scooter rental: €20–€35/day, Car: €35–€70/day
- Fuel: Around €2/litre

4. Activities & Entrance Fees:

- Museums: €3–€12
- Guided hiking or boat trips: €25–€100
- Beach entry: Mostly free, some charge for loungers (€5–€15/day)

Saving Tips Without Sacrificing Experience

- Travel in shoulder season (May–early June or mid-September): Lower prices, fewer crowds, great weather.
- Use public transportation and local ferries instead of taxis or charters.
- Eat where the locals eat—avoid the front-row restaurants on the port unless the menu looks genuinely Greek.
- Book early for accommodations and ferries during high season.
- Look for combo tickets for sites and museums.
- Share transport—many hotels can arrange shared airport or port transfers.
- Stay on lesser-known islands like Nisyros, Chalki, or Kasos for better value and unique charm.

Budget is personal. The real value comes from balancing comfort with authentic experience. Sometimes the €3 ouzo at a back-alley kafeneio brings more joy than a €50 dinner with a sunset view.

Booking Flights to the Dodecanese

Let's face it—getting to a Greek island sounds romantic, but it also requires a bit of savvy, especially if you want to skip long ferry rides or airport confusion. The good news is that Rhodes and Kos are both major regional air hubs, and once you're in the air, the Aegean opens up beautifully.

Main Airports in the Dodecanese

1. Rhodes International Airport (RHO) – "Diagoras"
   - Main international gateway
   - Year-round flights from Athens and Thessaloniki
   - Seasonal direct flights from many European cities
2. Kos International Airport (KGS) – "Hippocrates"
   - Another strong hub, especially in summer
   - Direct flights from northern Europe during peak season
3. Smaller Island Airports:
   - Karpathos (AOK), Kalymnos (JKL), Astypalea (JTY), and Leros (LRS) have domestic flights mainly from Athens.

Tip: Use Athens (ATH) as your launchpad. Olympic Air, Sky Express, and Aegean Airlines offer frequent, short domestic hops.

Flight Booking Strategies

Book Early for Summer (June–August):

- Direct international flights to Rhodes and Kos fill fast. Booking 3–6 months in advance is best.

Be Flexible with Dates:

- Flights to Rhodes and Kos vary wildly in price. Midweek flights tend to be cheaper. Use tools like Google Flights, Sky scanner, or Hopper to track fare drops.

Bundle & Save:

- Many airlines (like Aegean) offer multi-city or ferry/flight combos, ideal for island-hopping.

Alternative Routes:

- If flying to a smaller island (like Leros or Kasos), consider flying to Rhodes or Kos, then transferring via short domestic flight or ferry.
- Some travelers fly into Bodrum or Marmaris (Turkey) and take the fast ferry into Kos or Rhodes. It's scenic, affordable, and time-saving—but check visa needs.

Airlines That Frequently Serve the Dodecanese

Airline	Routes	Notes
Aegean Airlines	Athens → All major Dodecanese airports	Reliable, often includes free luggage
Sky Express	Domestic & regional	Smaller aircraft, efficient island connector
Ryanair	Seasonal international to Rhodes & Kos	Budget option—watch luggage fees
EasyJet	UK, Germany → Rhodes, Kos (seasonal)	Budget-friendly with many options
Lufthansa, TUI, Jet2, Transavia	European hubs → Rhodes/Kos (summer)	Often part of package holidays

Final Advice:

- Plan arrival and departure points carefully. You don't need to return to the same island you landed on. Many travelers fly into Rhodes and depart from Kos—or vice versa.
- Allow ferry-buffer time if connecting flights and ferries. Island weather can occasionally delay departures.
- Double-check your flight times and transfers when booking multiple stops. Greek islands reward flexible, curious travelers.

Ferries, Airlines & Inter-Island Transportation

In the Dodecanese, transportation isn't just a means to an end—it's part of the experience. Whether you're watching the sun rise from a slow ferry's deck or catching a quick hop to an isolated island, how you move between the islands shapes your journey. The key is knowing how to mix speed, scenery, and strategy.

A. Ferries: The Classic Way to Island Hop

Ferries are the lifeblood of the Dodecanese. They range from large overnight vessels with cabins to small passenger-only catamarans darting across turquoise waters.

Major Ferry Operators:

- **Blue Star Ferries** – Reliable, large ferries connecting Rhodes, Kos, Kalymnos, and more. Comfortable with cabins and vehicle options.
- **Dodekanisos Seaways** – Fast, efficient service between smaller islands (Lipsi, Symi, Kastellorizo, etc.).
- **Anek Lines, Sea Dreams, and LAFASI** – Smaller regional companies offering specific seasonal routes.

Popular Routes & Durations:

- Rhodes to Symi: ~1 hour (catamaran)
- Kos to Kalymnos: 35–50 minutes
- Rhodes to Karpathos: ~5–6 hours
- Patmos to Lipsi/Leros: ~1 hour

Tip: *Not all ferries run daily, especially outside peak season. Plan your route around ferry availability, not the other way around.*

Where to Book:

- Ferryhopper.com
- Direct Ferries
- Local travel agencies or kiosks (especially useful on smaller islands)

B. Inter-Island Flights

For longer hops or if you're tight on time, domestic flights offer speed and efficiency. Small regional airports connect key islands with each other and Athens.

Flight Connections (typically via Athens):

- Rhodes ↔ Karpathos, Kasos, Leros, Kalymnos
- Kos ↔ Rhodes, Leros (seasonal)

Sky Express and Olympic Air operate short, scenic flights that sometimes cost less than a cabin on an overnight ferry. But remember: luggage limits can be tight.

C. Local Transport on the Islands

Once you're on an island, getting around varies:

1. Car or Scooter Rental:

- Ideal for larger islands like Rhodes, Kos, or Karpathos.
- Scooters/ATVs are popular on smaller or mountainous islands.
- Always carry your international driving permit and be cautious on narrow, winding roads.

2. Public Buses:

- Most islands have seasonal bus routes connecting beaches, towns, and historic sites.
- Rhodes and Kos have reliable, frequent buses. Smaller islands often rely on 1–2 daily services.

3. Taxis:

- Convenient but costly on small islands. Few are metered, so agree on the fare in advance.

4. Water Taxis:

- Perfect for jumping between nearby beaches or islands like Symi ↔ Panormitis or Lipsi ↔ Aspronisia.
- Often run by locals—negotiate prices and schedules on-site.

What to Pack for Each Season & Island Type

Packing for the Dodecanese isn't just about swimsuits and sandals. The region's diversity in terrain, climate, and culture means your bag needs to adapt—whether you're temple-hopping in Lindos or hiking into the volcanic heart of Nisyros.

A. Essentials for All Seasons

- Passport & Travel Documents
- Travel Insurance Papers
- Credit/Debit Cards + Cash in Euros
- Universal Power Adapter (Greece uses Type C & F, 230V)
- Water Bottle (refillable)
- Sunscreen (reef-safe if you'll be swimming)
- Sunglasses + Hat
- Medications + First-Aid Kit
- Swimsuit + Quick-Dry Towel
- Sandals & Comfortable Walking Shoes

B. Spring (April–June)

- Temperatures: 18–27°C (64–80°F)
- Expect wildflowers, pleasant hiking weather, and fewer crowds.

What to Pack:

- Light layers
- Waterproof windbreaker (island breezes can surprise you)
- Hiking shoes or trail sandals
- Scarf/shawl for monasteries and cooler evenings

C. Summer (July–August)

- Temperatures: 28–38°C (82–100°F)
- It's hot, sunny, and crowded—hydration and sun protection are key.

What to Pack:

- Lightweight, breathable clothing (linen/cotton)
- Extra swimwear
- Aloe vera or after-sun lotion
- Sun hat with wide brim
- Foldable tote or beach bag
- Snorkelling gear (optional but fun!)

D. Autumn (September–October)

- Temperatures: 22–30°C (71–86°F)
- Still warm and ideal for both beach lounging and hiking.

What to Pack:

- Similar to spring
- Light sweater or hoodie for cooler nights
- Long pants for evenings or temple visits

E. Winter (November–March)

- Temperatures: 10–18°C (50–65°F)
- Fewer ferries, quiet villages, and some seasonal closures.

What to Pack:

- Warm layers
- Waterproof jacket or coat
- Closed shoes or boots
- Umbrella (just in case)

Packing smart means packing light—but also right. Always check what's available on your specific islands. For example, Nisyros has volcanic terrain, while Kastellorizo's appeal is its calm waterfront walks.

Travel Insurance, Connectivity & Essential Apps

Travel in the Dodecanese is usually safe, smooth, and soulful. But unexpected delays, lost luggage, ferry strikes, or injuries can happen, especially when island-hopping. And while you'll likely unplug, it helps to have the right digital tools at your fingertips.

A. Travel Insurance: What You Need

Don't skimp here. A few euros a day could save hundreds—or more—in emergencies.

What to Look for:

- Medical Coverage, including emergency evacuation
- Trip Cancellation/Interruption (especially if ferry schedules change)
- Lost/Stolen Luggage coverage
- Adventure Activities (for scuba diving, hiking, etc.)
- COVID-19 Related Cancellations or Treatment (still relevant in some cases)

Popular Providers:

- World Nomads
- Safety Wing
- Allianz Travel
- AXA Schengen

Tip: Always save digital and printed copies of your policy, ID, and claims contacts.

B. Staying Connected

Wi-Fi is decent across most islands, especially in hotels and cafés, but rural and remote beaches or ferry terminals may have limited access.

Your Options:

- Local SIM Card – Available at airports or kiosks. Vodafone, Cosmote, and WIND offer reliable service with prepaid tourist packages.

- eSIM – Easy digital setup if your phone supports it.
- Roaming – If you're from the EU, roaming is generally included at no extra charge.

C. Must-Have Travel Apps for the Dodecanese

App	Why It's Essential
Ferryhopper	Book/check ferry schedules in real-time
Google Maps / Maps.me	Offline maps + walking trails
XE Currency	Real-time conversion + tracking
Greek Travel Pages (GTP)	Local transport updates
AllTrails / Wikiloc	Hiking maps for islands like Karpathos and Nisyros
WhatsApp / Viber	Messaging and calls (especially for local drivers or guesthouses)
Google Translate	Great for menus and small conversations
Booking.com / Airbnb	Reliable local lodging, especially last-minute

In the Dodecanese, you're never far from help—or a good story. But being prepared with the right coverage, tools, and digital safety net lets you focus on what really matters: exploring, tasting, hiking, and dreaming freely.

CHAPTER

3

Where to Stay

Accommodation Overview by Island & Budget

When it comes to the Dodecanese, where you stay becomes part of the journey—not just a place to sleep. The islands offer everything from luxury resorts in Rhodes to quiet family-run pensions on Lipsi and seaside villas on Karpathos. The secret to a memorable experience? Choosing a place that matches your travel style, pace, and expectations.

A. Budget Ranges: What You Get

€ (Budget / Backpacker)

- Dorm beds, guesthouses, family-run pensions
- Basic but clean, often with shared bathrooms
- Local hospitality and location over luxury
- Price Range: €20–€50/night

€€ (Mid-Range)

- Boutique hotels, well-reviewed B&Bs, modern apartments
- Comfortable amenities, often with breakfast included
- Central or beachfront locations
- Price Range: €55–€120/night

€€€ (Luxury)

- Upscale resorts, private villas, heritage hotels
- Pools, spas, concierge, sea views
- Often includes gourmet dining and private beaches
- Price Range: €130–€400+/night

Tip: Prices are higher in July–August and lower in shoulder seasons (May–June, Sept–Oct). Book early if traveling in high summer.

B. Island-by-Island Accommodation Guide

Rhodes

- Budget: *Stay Hostel, Hotel Parthenon* – Walking distance to Rhodes Old Town.
- Mid-Range: *Spirit of the Knights Boutique Hotel* – Eco-luxury meets medieval charm.
- Luxury: *Lindos Blu, Atrium Prestige Thalasso* – Ocean-facing suites and elite service.

Kos

- Budget: *Catherine Hotel* – Near the port and beaches.
- Mid-Range: *Kos Aktis Art Hotel* – Sleek design with waterfront balconies.
- Luxury: *Michelangelo Resort & Spa* – Infinity pool with panoramic views.

Symi

- Budget: *Nireus Hotel* – Charming neoclassical on the harbor.
- Mid-Range: *Opera House Hotel* – Quiet garden setting, 5 mins from the quay.
- Luxury: *The Old Markets* – Boutique glam in a historic merchant house.

Karpathos

- Budget: *Irene's House* – Self-catering, close to beaches.
- Mid-Range: *Alimounda Mare Hotel* – Excellent family services, pools.
- Luxury: *Arhontiko Hotel* – Traditional stone-built property with sea views.

Leros

- Budget: *Tony's Rooms* – Simple, central, and steps from the beach.
- Mid-Range: *Castle Vigla* – Apartments with panoramic sea views.
- Luxury: *Crithoni's Paradise Hotel* – Pool, spa, and private balconies.

Patmos

- Budget: *Blue Bay Hotel* – Sea views and genuine Greek breakfast.
- Mid-Range: *Petra Hotel & Suites* – Elegant and understated.
- Luxury: *Patmos Aktis Suites & Spa* – Five-star, on a divine beach.

Smaller Islands (Lipsi, Tilos, Kastellorizo, Nisyros)

- Mostly mid-range and budget options run by locals.
- Expect personal touches, local cuisine, and slower rhythms.
- Villas and homes often available via Airbnb or Booking.com.

Story insight: I once stayed in a rustic guesthouse on Nisyros with no air conditioning, but the owner served warm bread at dawn and gave me directions to a hidden hot spring. That was worth more than any five-star check-in.

C. Booking Tips by Traveller Type

- Solo Travelers: Look for hostels in Rhodes or Kos, or family-run pensions in Symi for connection and safety.
- Couples: Boutique hotels in Lindos or romantic waterfront studios in Patmos.

- Groups: Villas in Karpathos or apartments in Leros offer space and savings.
- Off-the-Beaten-Path: Choose Nisyros, Kastellorizo, or Tilos for total tranquillity

Family-Friendly Hotels, Villas & Apartments

Traveling the Dodecanese with kids? You're in for a treat. Many islands are naturally family-friendly, with safe beaches, welcoming locals, and accommodations designed with families in mind. Whether you're looking for a self-catering apartment, a resort with kids' clubs, or a village villa for multigenerational reunions, there's something here for every family size and style.

A. What Makes a Stay Family-Friendly in the Dodecanese?

- Proximity to calm, shallow beaches
- Rooms or apartments with kitchenettes
- On-site playgrounds or child-safe pools
- Flexible meal options or half-board packages
- Availability of cribs, high chairs, or babysitting

In Greek culture, children are seen as a blessing—not a nuisance. Don't be surprised if taverna owners bring free juice or dessert for your kids.

B. Recommended Family Stays by Island

Rhodes

- *Labranda Blue Bay Resort* (Ialyssos): Waterslides, pools, playgrounds, direct beach access.
- *Grecotel Lux Me Dama Dama*: All-inclusive and designed for kids and teens.
- *Lindian Jewel*: Smaller hotel near gentle beaches with family suites.

Kos

- *Neptune Hotels – Resort, Convention Centre & Spa*: Huge, clean, tons of family activities.
- *Kipriotis Village Resort*: Perfect for children with multiple pools and mini-clubs.
- *Mythos Apartments* (Tigaki): Budget-friendly, steps from a sandy beach.

Karpathos

- *Villas Lefkothea*: Family-run, full kitchens, mountain views.
- *Alkioni Hotel* (Finiki): Quiet, safe, and walking distance to beach and tavernas.
- *Royal Beach Hotel*: A blend of comfort and beach proximity.

Leros

- *Archontiko Angelou*: Feels like a storybook home, with gardens and lots of space.
- *Alidian Bay Suites*: Modern apartments with kitchenettes and beach access.

Patmos

- *Skala Hotel*: Near harbor, family rooms, great pool.
- *Patmos Paradise Hotel*: Close to the island's best beach, Kampos, with babysitting services.

Symi

- *Emporio Studios*: Quiet cove, spacious rooms, and a safe swimming spot.
- *Pedi Beach Hotel*: Ideal for younger children, calm waters, and warm hosts.

C. Villas & Apartments for Families

Sometimes, space and flexibility beat room service. Here's where private villas and apartments shine, especially for larger families or longer stays.

- Airbnb/VRBO: Offer countless family homes with kitchens, laundry, and outdoor play areas.
- Top Family Villa Destinations: Rhodes (Lindos, Faliraki), Kos (Kefalos, Zia), Karpathos (Arkasa), Leros (Agia Marina).

Pro tip: Look for properties with washer/dryer access—it saves luggage space and mid-trip stress.

D. Family Travel Tips for the Dodecanese

- Avoid late-night ferry transfers with little kids.
- Bring snacks and sun protection at all times.
- Choose islands with hospitals or medical centres for peace of mind (Rhodes, Kos, Kalymnos).
- Strollers may struggle on hilly or cobbled island terrain—consider a backpack carrier for toddlers.

Romantic Getaways & Boutique Stays

The Dodecanese might not make the headlines like Santorini when it comes to honeymoons, but that's precisely the charm—it's more intimate, more authentic, and far less crowded. Whether you're celebrating love or just escaping with someone special, these islands offer candlelit dinners, azure views, hidden beaches, and soul-soothing serenity.

A. What Makes a Stay Romantic Here?

- Sunset views from your private balcony
- Boutique hotels tucked into quiet harbours or medieval lanes
- Private dining on beach terraces
- Authentic touches like stone walls, olive-wood furniture, and lavender gardens

There's something deeply romantic about wandering through an empty cobbled street in Symi at twilight, the lamps glowing gold and the Aegean lapping against the quay.

B. Island Recommendations for Romance

Symi

Charming neoclassical mansions, pastel houses, and an air of faded glamour.

- *Stay at:* The Old Markets – Chic luxury in a renovated 18th-century trading hall.
- *Do:* Sunset dinner at Tholos overlooking the harbor.

Patmos

Sacred, silent, and impossibly beautiful.

- *Stay at:* Petra Hotel & Suites – Terrace views of the Aegean, minimalist elegance.
- *Do:* Walk hand in hand through Hora, one of the most romantic old towns in Greece.

Leros

Undiscovered, with sweeping coastal walks and Art Deco architecture.

- *Stay at:* Alinda Hotel or Crithoni's Paradise Hotel.
- *Do:* Private boat tour to the blue cave and deserted beaches.

Rhodes (Lindos)

While busy, Lindos has retained its magic.

- *Stay at:* Melenos Lindos – Rooftop breakfasts and rooms carved into cliffs.
- *Do:* Dine under the stars at Tambakio, on the sand of St. Paul's Bay.

Kastellorizo

Tiny, remote, and perfect for two.

- *Stay at:* Poseidon Hotel – A few steps from the harbor.
- *Do:* Swim alone in the Blue Grotto. It feels like the world belongs to you.

C. Romance Tips in the Dodecanese

- Book outside of July–August for peace and better prices.
- Request rooms with sea views, private terraces, or jacuzzis.
- Many hotels offer special honeymoon or anniversary packages—email ahead!

Unique Lodgings: Windmills, Historic Homes & Monastery Guesthouses

Looking for more than a standard hotel? The Dodecanese is filled with extraordinary places to stay, each offering a powerful sense of place. Here, you can sleep in a windmill overlooking the Aegean, a restored captain's house, or even a monastery-turned-guesthouse that whispers centuries of history.

A. Stay in a Windmill

Once used to grind grain with the wind, these iconic structures have been converted into charming, round-shaped accommodations with spiral staircases, panoramic views, and a rustic feel.

- Rhodes: The Windmill Villa near Fanes – stylishly restored with a private garden.
- Leros: Traditional Windmill of Agia Marina – stone-built with unforgettable sunsets.

Sleeping in a windmill isn't just about the novelty—it's about waking up and seeing the island unfold in a 360° panorama as the light changes.

B. Historic Homes & Neoclassical Mansions

Many locals have transformed their ancestral homes into boutique lodgings, preserving architectural features while adding modern comfort.

- Symi: Neoclassical homes near the harbor—high ceilings, frescoed walls, marble staircases.
- Kastellorizo: Elegant stone houses with wooden balconies that jut over the sea.
- Kalymnos (Pothia): Old sponge merchant houses that blend history with hospitality.

C. Monastery Guesthouses & Spiritual Retreats

The Dodecanese islands are deeply spiritual, and some monasteries offer simple guest accommodations for those seeking quiet or reflection.

- Patmos: Monastery of Evangelismos – Simple, serene, and welcoming (modest attire required).

- Nisyros: Panagia Spiliani Monastery – Rare to stay here, but worth asking locally.
- Tilos: Agios Panteleimon Monastery – Occasionally opens for overnight stays during festivals.

Staying in a monastery is not a luxury experience. But the peace, the silence, and the feeling of timelessness can be more valuable than five-star fluff.

D. Booking & Etiquette Tips for Unique Lodgings

- Reserve well in advance, especially for windmills and monastery stays.
- Be respectful of religious customs in monastery accommodations.
- Expect some quirks and limitations: low ceilings, antique furniture, or no air-con—but that's part of the charm.

Long-Stay & Digital Nomad Options

The Dodecanese isn't just for short getaways. With mild winters, friendly locals, reliable Wi-Fi, and lower costs, the region has emerged as a quiet paradise for digital nomads, slow travelers, and long-stay wanderers. Whether you're working remotely or spending a few months escaping the grind, this cluster of islands offers what few others can: beauty without burnout.

A. Why the Dodecanese Works for Long Stays

- Affordable rent outside of peak summer months
- Diverse environments—work one month by a beach, another in a mountain village
- Relaxed pace of life that enhances productivity and well-being

- Increasing number of co-working cafes and high-speed Wi-Fi locations
- Greece's digital nomad visa and extended-stay options

B. Best Islands for Digital Nomads & Long-Term Travelers

Rhodes (City & Lindos)

- Best infrastructure and year-round life
- Multiple coworking cafes and stable internet
- Winter is quiet but services remain open

Kos

- Vibrant local community
- Biking culture makes daily life simple and healthy
- Popular with long-stay Germans and Dutch, so easy to find expat support

Kalymnos

- Climbing community creates a creative, global vibe
- Great for active nomads looking to combine work and adrenaline

Leros & Patmos

- Slower, quieter lifestyle
- Ideal for writers, designers, and creatives
- Lower rent and strong local hospitality

C. Where to Live: Apartments, Studios, Homestays

- Apartments: Many locals offer long-term rentals between October and May.
- Studios: Budget-friendly, especially in inland villages.
- Homestays: Great for cultural immersion—many families offer "room and board" in exchange for light help or payment.

D. Practical Tips for Long-Term Life in the Dodecanese

- Sim Cards: COSMOTE or Vodafone offer excellent data plans.
- Utilities: Check if utilities are included in rent—some older homes may need heating in winter.
- Visa Info: EU citizens have no issues; others can apply for Greece's digital nomad visa (minimum income required).
- Community: Join Facebook groups like "Expats in Rhodes" or "Digital Nomads Greece" for support.

The Dodecanese isn't flashy. But for those who value authenticity, daily beauty, and slow, meaningful travel—it's one of the best-kept secrets in the Mediterranean.

CHAPTER

4

Island-by-Island Guide

Group A – Must-Visit Icons

The Dodecanese archipelago isn't just a scattering of islands in the Aegean—it's a mosaic of histories, landscapes, and stories that stretch across centuries. Within this group of twelve main islands and many more islets, there are a few that stand as undisputed icons—the crown jewels of the Dodecanese. These are the must-visits. They aren't just popular—they're unforgettable.

In this section, we explore three of the most evocative islands in the region: Rhodes, Kos, and Patmos. Each has a distinctive personality, and knowing what they offer—and how to experience them well— can elevate your trip from good to unforgettable.

A. Rhodes – Medieval Old Town, Beaches & Culture

Rhodes is often the first stop for Dodecanese explorers, and for good reason. It's the largest island in the group, a cultural powerhouse, and a place where ancient, medieval, and modern worlds collide under the Aegean sun.

Why Visit Rhodes?

Rhodes offers layers of history, a UNESCO-listed Old Town, long golden beaches, lively nightlife, charming mountain villages, and enough diversity to satisfy a wide range of traveller types—from beach lovers to culture seekers.

Highlights & Experiences

1. The Medieval City of Rhodes (Old Town)

- One of the best-preserved medieval towns in Europe.
- Walk through the Street of the Knights, visit the Palace of the Grand Master, and explore tiny alleyways filled with artisan shops and hidden cafes.
- A dream for photographers, history buffs, and romantics alike.

2. Lindos: The Whitewashed Cliffside Gem

- A stunning whitewashed village crowned by an ancient acropolis.
- Climb to the Acropolis of Lindos for panoramic sea views.
- Enjoy the clear waters of St. Paul's Bay below—ideal for swimming and kayaking.

3. Beaches of Every Kind

- Anthony Quinn Bay: Turquoise water in a rocky cove.
- Tsambika Beach: Wide, sandy, and great for families.
- Prasonisi: A surfer's paradise where two seas meet.

4. Ancient Ruins

- Kamiros: A "Greek Pompeii," offering insight into ancient urban planning.
- Ialysos and Filerimos Hill: Ruins with epic vistas.

Who Should Go to Rhodes?

- First-time travelers: It's the best base to start understanding the Dodecanese.

- Families: Beach resorts, shallow swimming areas, and kid-friendly towns.
- History lovers: From ancient Greece to medieval knights.
- Nightlife seekers: Faliraki and Rhodes Town have bars, clubs, and sunset lounges.

Insider Tips

- Avoid peak Old Town crowds by arriving before 10 a.m. or after 5 p.m.
- The eastern coast is calmer and better for swimming.
- Consider renting a car to explore inland villages like Embonas or Monolithos.

B. Kos – Healing History & Vibrant Coastline

If Rhodes is the cultural capital, Kos is the healer, blending wellness heritage with modern energy. Known as the island of Hippocrates, Kos is a fantastic blend of ancient ruins, energetic towns, long beaches, and bike-friendly charm.

Why Visit Kos?

Kos has a little of everything: history, health, and hedonism. It's the kind of place where you can explore ancient temples in the morning, sunbathe in the afternoon, and dance until dawn—if that's your thing.

Highlights & Experiences

1. Asklepion of Kos

- An ancient healing center and the birthplace of Western medicine.
- Walk where Hippocrates himself taught and treated.

- Offers breath-taking views over the island and across to Turkey.

2. Kos Town

- Lively but laid-back, filled with historic ruins, a Venetian castle, and harbor promenades.
- Visit the Tree of Hippocrates, the ancient Agora, and the Casa Romana (Roman villa).

3. Thermal Springs at Agios Fokas

- Natural hot springs right on the beach.
- Open 24/7 and free to enter—perfect for stargazing soaks.

4. Beaches & Bike Culture

- Kos is bike-friendly, with designated lanes and flat terrain.
- Tigaki Beach: Wide, white sands great for families.
- Kefalos: More remote and relaxed, with dramatic cliffs and turquoise waters.

<u>Who Should Go to Kos?</u>

- Health and wellness travelers: Spa culture, natural springs, and history of medicine.
- Younger crowds and solo travelers: Good nightlife and social hostels.
- Cyclists: Best island in the Dodecanese for biking.
- Families: Flat terrain, calm beaches, and lots of child-friendly attractions.

Insider Tips

- Kos Town can be lively and loud—choose accommodation a few kilometres out for quieter nights.
- Explore inland villages like Zia for mountain views and stunning sunsets.
- Visit the islet of Kastri—a postcard-perfect rock with a tiny chapel.

C. Patmos – Spiritual Island of the Apocalypse

Patmos is unlike anywhere else in the Dodecanese. Revered by Christians as the island where St. John received the Revelation, Patmos blends spiritual mystique, austere beauty, and intellectual charm. It's not a party island—it's a place for reflection, beauty, and deep cultural connection.

Why Visit Patmos?

Because it's timeless. Patmos invites you to slow down, breathe deeply, and feel connected to something bigger—whether that's the divine, the past, or simply yourself.

Highlights & Experiences

1. Cave of the Apocalypse

- A UNESCO World Heritage site.
- The very spot where St. John is said to have received the visions recorded in the Book of Revelation.
- A powerful spiritual experience even for non-religious visitors.

2. Monastery of Saint John the Theologian

- Towers over the island like a fortress.

- Home to rare icons, manuscripts, and a still-active monastic community.
- The view from the top is breath-taking—both for its history and panoramas.

3. Hora – The Most Beautiful Village in the Dodecanese

- Maze-like alleyways, noble mansions, hidden squares.
- Atmosphere is dignified yet relaxed.
- Many come to Patmos just to stay in Hora and never leave.

4. Beaches of Simplicity

- Psili Ammos: A 30-minute hike rewards you with silky sand and silence.
- Lambi Beach: Known for its colorful pebbles.
- Grikos Bay: Calm, pretty, and perfect for contemplative swims.

Who Should Go to Patmos?

- Spiritual travelers: Pilgrims and seekers alike find peace here.
- Couples: For quiet romance, away from the mainstream.
- Writers and creatives: Many come here to think, retreat, and create.
- Cultural purists: Few places offer such depth without distraction.

Insider Tips

- Patmos has no airport—you'll need to ferry from Kos, Leros, or Samos.
- Stay in Hora if you're after atmosphere; Skala for convenience.

- Bring comfortable walking shoes—exploring on foot is the only way to go.

Group B: Colorful Harbors & Neoclassical Charm

The Dodecanese archipelago isn't only about large islands packed with medieval castles or famous beaches. There's another side—a softer, more elegant and artistic realm of colorful facades, tranquil harbor, and sun-drenched neoclassical architecture. This is where Group B islands shine.

Here, we step into two of the most painterly and poetic destinations in the Dodecanese: Symi and Chalki. Both are postcard-perfect in different ways—Symi exudes upscale glamour and tradition, while Chalki is serenity incarnate. These islands offer charm in soft hues, slow rhythms, and timeless grace.

A. Symi – Glamour Meets Tradition

Symi is the jewel box of the Dodecanese—a little island with big personality. As your ferry pulls into Gialos Harbor, the view is almost cinematic: tiered neoclassical mansions, painted in rose, buttercup, and mint green, rise up the hills like a pastel amphitheater.

Why Visit Symi?

Symi is for those who travel with their eyes wide open—for the aesthetes, the romantics, the artists, and the wanderers. It's glamorous without being showy, traditional without being sleepy. And while it may be small, it never feels limited.

Highlights & Experiences

1. Gialos Harbor: The Iconic Arrival

- Possibly the most photogenic harbor in Greece.
- Colorful 19th-century mansions reflect on the sapphire sea.
- Waterfront lined with boutiques, bakeries, and family-run tavernas.

2. Chorio (Symi Town's Upper District)

- Climb the 500-step Kali Strata to reach this sleepy, authentic village.
- Discover quiet squares, faded mansions, and tiny churches.
- The views back down to the harbor are worth the leg workout.

3. Monastery of Archangel Michael Panormitis

- Located on the opposite side of the island, reachable by boat or road.
- A pilgrimage site famous for its miraculous icon and tranquil setting.
- Blends religious heritage with peaceful scenery—don't miss the frescoes.

4. Beaches of Crystal & Quiet

- Nanou Beach: Long, pebbled, turquoise waters—arrive by boat.
- Agia Marina: Beach club vibes with parasols and water taxis.
- Marathounda: Clear waters and goats that roam the shoreline.

Who Should Go to Symi?

- Couples and honeymooners: Dreamlike settings and boutique stays.
- Luxury travelers: Upscale dining, chic rentals, and yacht culture.
- Photographers and artists: The light, architecture, and colors are irresistible.
- Island hoppers: Close to Rhodes, making it a perfect short escape.

Insider Tips

- Day-trippers from Rhodes often crowd the harbor midday—explore early morning or late evening for the most magical moments.
- Hire a private water taxi to reach more remote beaches.
- Dine at To Spitiko or Taverna Tholos for fresh seafood with views.

B. Chalki – Laid-Back Luxury in Pastel Paradise

If Symi is a glamorous muse, Chalki (or Halki) is her quieter, introspective sister. This island is all about elegant stillness, pastel beauty, and a pace so slow it feels sacred.

Chalki may be small, but it has a soul far bigger than its square kilometres suggest.

Why Visit Chalki?

Because you need an island that asks nothing of you. There are no nightclubs. No crowded tourist zones. Just a small, breathtakingly pretty harbor, a few divine beaches, and the permission to rest.

Highlights & Experiences

1. Emborio (Chalki Town)

- The island's only village, and one of the most beautiful harbors in Greece.
- Brightly coloured houses reflect on the water like an impressionist painting.
- Locals greet you by name after one day. Time seems to pool here.

2. Nimborio Beaches & Swimming Spots

- Ftenagia Beach: A short walk from town, with sunbeds and café service.
- Pondamos Beach: Shallow, safe, and sandy—perfect for families.
- Kania Beach: Remote feel, reachable by foot or boat.

3. Monastery of Agios Ioannis Alargas

- Hidden in the island's interior, accessed by hike or boat.
- Peaceful, off-grid, and spiritually rich.
- Hosts a major festival in August where people sleep outdoors under the stars.

4. Old Chalki & Abandoned Villages

- Hike to the now-deserted village of Chorio, where ruins whisper of past centuries.
- Stop by the medieval castle of the Knights of St. John, offering panoramic views.

Who Should Go to Chalki?

- Digital detoxers and mindfulness seekers.
- Romantics who want an unhurried escape.
- Families with young children: Safe, slow, and sweet.
- Solo travelers: You'll never feel alone here—Chalki makes space for you.

Insider Tips

- Arrive via ferry from Rhodes—it's the simplest route.
- Bring cash: Many businesses don't accept cards.
- Book accommodation early—limited boutique guesthouses fill up quickly.

Symi vs. Chalki – Snapshot Comparison

Feature	Symi	Chalki
Ambience	Glamorous, vibrant, photogenic	Peaceful, contemplative, pastel-perfect
Best For	Couples, photographers, culture lovers	Solo travelers, families, digital detox
Access	Day ferries from Rhodes & other islands	Primarily via Rhodes by ferry
Beaches	Best reached by water taxi	Walkable, more accessible beaches
Architecture	Neoclassical mansions, dramatic terrain	Compact harbor village, gentle hills

Group C: Nature, Adventure & Hiking

There's a wild pulse beating beneath the sun-kissed beauty of the Dodecanese—a rhythm heard in the wind-sculpted cliffs, ancient goat trails, pine-covered mountains, and untouched coastlines. Group C islands are for the explorers, the hikers, the nature-lovers, and the quietly courageous travelers who find their joy beyond the guidebook gloss.

Here we journey into Kalymnos, Karpathos, and Tilos—each offering a unique blend of raw landscapes, outdoor thrills, and off-the-grid authenticity.

A. Kalymnos – Rock Climbing & Sponge Diving

Kalymnos is rugged and resilient, both in terrain and spirit. It's a place where mountains fall sharply into an electric-blue sea, and cliffs stretch like ancient walls—ideal for adventurers who crave adrenaline over Aperol. But beneath its craggy face lies a cultural richness shaped by the sea: Kalymnos is also the island of the sponge divers—once legendary, now traditional, still proud.

"I came for the climbing. I stayed for the people—and the stories carved into every stone."

Rock Climber's Paradise

Kalymnos is world-renowned among climbers, boasting over 3,400 bolted routes across limestone crags and overhangs. Whether you're a total novice or a seasoned climber, you'll find a vertical playground with global fame.

- **Best Climbing Areas:** Grande Grotta, Odyssey, Sikati Cave (a cathedral-like collapsed roof), and Arginonta.

- **Season**: Spring and autumn are perfect—cooler temps and fewer crowds.
- **Local Tip:** The Kalymnos Climbing Festival (usually in October) attracts top international climbers and offers workshops, competitions, and unforgettable energy.

History in the Deep: Sponge Diving Legacy

Kalymnos's deep waters made it a global hub for natural sponge diving in the 19th and early 20th centuries. Though synthetic sponges changed the industry, the heritage still thrives.

- Visit the Sponge Factory Museums in Pothia Town for exhibitions, tools, and diving suits that look like space gear from another era.
- Meet local divers who continue the tradition and offer storytelling tours—like stepping into an oral epic.

Beaches & Blue Adventures

- Plati Gialos: A quiet black-sand beach with a dramatic backdrop.
- Massouri: The go-to for climbing basecamp, beach lounging, and cafés.
- Pothia: A harbor town full of charm, color, and lively tavernas.

Ideal For

- Climbers and mountaineers
- Travelers wanting cultural depth beyond the beach
- Adventure-seekers and off-season explorers

"Kalymnos doesn't show off—but if you're looking for adventure with soul, this island gives more than you bargained for."

B. Karpathos – Untamed Trails & Local Villages

Karpathos is a landscape carved by myth and wind—dramatic, remote, and rooted in centuries-old traditions. It's a place of craggy ridges, mountain trails, and time-frozen villages. The island feels like the Dodecanese's secret stash—huge, under-touristic, and wild in all the right ways.

"On Karpathos, the wind tells stories. And if you hike far enough, the mountains start answering back."

Hiking Heaven

Karpathos is a walker's wonderland, with marked trails weaving through pine forests, hills, and along cliff-lined coasts.

- **Top Trails:**
    - Olympos to Avlona: An old stone path connecting ancient mountain villages.
    - Lefkos to Lastos: Coastal views and peaceful forest sections.
    - Diafani Loop: A mix of nature and tradition ending at a fishing port.
- **Pro Tips:** Spring and fall offer the best temperatures. Bring hiking boots—this terrain isn't casual flip-flop country.

Village Time Travel

Some of Karpathos's villages feel like you've entered a parallel time dimension. The most famous, Olympos, is an ethereal hilltop hamlet where women still wear traditional dresses daily and bake in wood ovens.

- Olympos: A living folk museum perched in the clouds.
- Mesochori & Aperi: Known for flower-draped balconies and unhurried cafés.

- Pigadia: The modern main town, perfect for basecamp and supplies.

Untouched Beaches

- Apella: Consistently ranked among Greece's best beaches.
- Kira Panagia: Dreamy waters framed by mountains.
- Ahata: Secluded and favoured by locals.

Ideal For

- Serious hikers and mountain bikers
- Cultural explorers and photographers
- Travelers craving solitude and tradition

"You don't find Karpathos. It finds you—when you're finally ready to let nature and tradition be the guide."

C. Tilos – Eco-Conscious Island Life

Tilos is tiny but mighty—the Dodecanese's green pioneer. This island leads the way in eco-tourism, renewable energy, and preserving natural biodiversity. It's also hauntingly beautiful, quietly spiritual, and proudly different.

"Tilos isn't the loudest island, but it may just be the most visionary."

Greece's Green Trailblazer

Tilos was the first island in the Mediterranean to operate entirely on wind and solar energy. Environmental awareness here isn't a slogan—it's a lifestyle.

- Tilos Energy Project: Award-winning sustainability initiative.

- Plastic-free initiatives and a strong focus on local, seasonal food.

Birdwatcher's Bliss

Tilos is a designated Natura 2000 site with over 150 species of resident and migratory birds. Bring your binoculars—falcons, herons, and even Bonelli's eagles circle the skies.

- Best spots: Livadia wetlands, Eristos valley, and the mountain ridges above Mikro Chorio.

Hiker's Dream

- Livadia to Mikro Chorio: Passes ghost villages and olive groves.
- Agios Antonios loop: Coastal serenity and panoramic views.
- Hiking Festival in May: Celebrates the island's walking heritage with guided treks.

Paleontological Surprise

- Visit the Tilos Museum of Dwarf Elephants—yes, really.
- In a cave near Megalo Chorio, scientists discovered bones of miniature elephants that lived here until 4,000 BC.

Remote Beaches

- Eristos Beach: Wide, unspoiled, and perfect for campers and naturists.
- Agios Antonios: Remote and best accessed on foot.
- Lethra Beach: Pebbled cove reached by scenic path.

Ideal For

- Eco-conscious travelers
- Birdwatchers and hikers
- Slow travelers and digital detoxers

"Tilos doesn't shout. It whispers truth: that sustainable travel isn't a trend—it's the future. And it starts with places like this."

Quick Comparison Table: Group C Islands

Island	Signature Activities	Atmosphere	Ideal For
Kalymnos	Rock climbing, sponge diving	Rugged & adventurous	Climbers, culture seekers
Karpathos	Hiking, mountain villages	Wild & traditional	Hikers, solitude seekers, photographers
Tilos	Eco-tourism, birdwatching	Peaceful & visionary	Nature lovers, slow travelers, eco-tourists

Group D: Remote & Authentic Escapes

For travelers seeking refuge from crowds and a chance to immerse themselves in unfiltered island life, the Dodecanese offers some of its best-kept secrets in its more remote corners. These islands are less about flashy tourist draws and more about authenticity, slow rhythms, and stories carved by time. Welcome to Group D—where you'll find Nisyros and Leros, islands that embody the quiet beauty of discovery, history, and nature far from the beaten path.

A. Nisyros – Volcanic Landscapes & Hilltop Villages

Nisyros is one of the most geologically fascinating islands in Greece, a place where you can literally walk on the moon — or at least on an active volcano's edge. This small island is a rare blend of natural wonder and traditional charm, where ancient villages cling to hillsides and volcanic craters steam in the midday sun.

Exploring the Volcano

The island's most famous attraction—and for many the reason to visit—is the Nisyros volcano, one of the youngest in the Aegean and still active.

- **Stefanos Crater:** A massive volcanic caldera with fumaroles and steaming vents you can approach safely, filling the air with sulphurous scents.
- **Guided Hikes:** Trails wind through volcanic craters and volcanic rock formations, providing otherworldly landscapes unlike anywhere else in the Dodecanese.
- **Volcanological Museum:** In Mandraki, this small but rich museum explains the island's geological evolution with models, rocks, and photographs.

Hilltop Villages & Traditional Life

Nisyros's villages feel like postcard-perfect snapshots of Greece's past.

- Mandraki: The charming capital, home to the harbor, cobbled streets, and the impressive 14th-century Castle of the Knights overlooking the sea.
- Nikía: A breathtakingly perched village with narrow alleys, traditional architecture, and stunning views over the crater.
- Emporios: Known for its local pottery workshops and quiet beaches.

- Local Traditions: The island preserves many religious festivals and folk customs that travelers can witness or participate in, especially during the summer months.

Beaches & Nature

- **Pelekita Beach:** A volcanic black-sand beach that's strikingly different from the usual white sands elsewhere.
- **Ladiko Bay:** Secluded and crystal-clear waters, perfect for snorkelling.
- **Thermal Springs:** Natural hot springs near the village of Mandraki offer a relaxing, therapeutic experience in mineral-rich waters.

Food & Local Flavours

Nisyros's cuisine is a celebration of simple, fresh ingredients.

- Try roasted goat with local herbs, freshly caught seafood, and unique island cheeses.
- Visit family-run tavernas where recipes have been passed down for generations.
- Honey and almonds are specialties, often used in desserts and pastries.

Ideal For

- Geology enthusiasts and nature lovers
- Travelers craving peace and authentic village life
- Adventure seekers eager to hike volcanic terrain

"Walking the crater of Nisyros, you can almost hear the island breathing beneath your feet. It's an experience that changes the way you see nature—and yourself."

B. Leros – Hidden Histories & Peaceful Beaches

Leros is an island of quiet dignity, layered with rich, often overlooked history, and graced by peaceful, uncrowded beaches. Its unhurried pace invites travelers to slow down, stroll through quaint harbors, and reflect amid stunning natural beauty and cultural depth.

A Walk Through History

Leros has witnessed centuries of history, from Byzantine monasteries to World War II fortifications, and even Cold War bunkers. Its heritage is tangible at every corner.

- **Castle of Panteli:** Overlooking the main town, a medieval fortress with panoramic views and a sense of timelessness.
- **Alinda Bay**: Site of historical naval battles and serene today, perfect for contemplation.
- **Lakki Town:** Known for its unique Italian architecture from the 1930s, a living museum of interwar modernism.
- **World War II & Cold War Sites:** Explore abandoned tunnels, forts, and military installations—a raw reminder of the island's strategic importance.

Beaches for Every Mood

Unlike the bustling party beaches of some Dodecanese islands, Leros offers quiet, pristine shores where you can unwind in near solitude.

- **Alinda Beach:** Sandy, family-friendly, with calm shallow waters.
- **Agia Marina:** More secluded, surrounded by pine trees and perfect for swimming.
- **Vromolithos Bay:** A small fishing harbor with pebble beaches and traditional tavernas nearby.

- **Lefkos**: A small village with several quiet coves, ideal for snorkelling.

Authentic Island Life

Leros is famous for its welcoming locals who maintain strong ties to the sea and farming.

- Wander through small villages where life unfolds slowly, with daily markets, seaside cafés, and artisans.
- Seasonal festivals highlight local traditions—religious processions, music, and food celebrations fill the calendar.
- Try fresh octopus, homemade bread, and wine produced by small, family-run vineyards.

Outdoor Activities

- Hiking trails connect villages and ancient sites, often following the coastline with breath-taking views.
- Kayaking and sailing are popular ways to explore hidden coves.
- Birdwatching spots abound, with migratory species passing through in spring and autumn.

Ideal For

- History buffs and cultural explorers
- Families and travelers seeking tranquillity
- Outdoor enthusiasts looking for gentle hikes and water activities

"Leros feels like a cherished secret, where the past meets peaceful present and the sea sings the oldest songs."

Summary Comparison of Group D Islands

Island	Key Highlights	Vibe	Best For
Nisyros	Volcanic hikes, hilltop charm	Dramatic & traditional	Geology lovers, nature seekers
Leros	Historic sites, tranquil beaches	Quiet & authentic	History buffs, families, slow travelers

C. Kasos – Raw, Rustic, Real

Kasos is one of the most undiscovered islands in the Dodecanese, a place that truly lives up to the mantra of "off the beaten path." With a rugged landscape, strong traditions, and a pace that matches the sea's gentle rhythms, Kasos offers a rare, immersive experience in island life—raw and untouched by mass tourism.

"Kasos is not for the casual tourist. It's for the traveller who craves authenticity and the beauty of simplicity."

Untamed Natural Beauty

Kasos's terrain is dramatic—steep hills, rocky coasts, and quiet coves. The island's wild landscapes make it ideal for hikers and nature lovers.

- Hiking Trails: Explore ancient shepherd paths that connect small villages, olive groves, and hidden beaches.
- Secluded Beaches: Beaches like Agios Nikolaos and Marmari are pristine, often completely empty even in peak season.
- Marine Life: The waters around Kasos are excellent for snorkelling and diving, rich with Mediterranean Sea life.

Deeply Rooted Traditions

Kasos's culture remains robust, with many old-world customs still practiced daily.

- The island is known for its traditional music and dance, performed regularly in village squares.
- Local crafts such as weaving and embroidery keep centuries-old skills alive.
- Religious festivals, especially the Feast of the Assumption, are vibrant events where the community gathers in joyous celebration.

Kasos Town & Villages

- Fri is the main harbor and administrative center—quiet, with a handful of cafés and tavernas serving simple, fresh food.
- Villages like Myrties and Pachia Ammos showcase classic Kasian architecture: stone houses, narrow streets, and communal squares.
- Life here feels like stepping back in time, with friendly locals eager to share stories and invite visitors into their daily routines.

Cuisine

Kasos's food is grounded in local ingredients and centuries-old recipes.

- Try Kassopiako Cheese, a local specialty.
- Fresh seafood, wild greens, and traditional pies made from herbs and local cheeses.
- The island's honey and homemade liqueurs add sweetness and warmth to the culinary experience.

D. Astypalaia – Cycladic Charm with a Dodecanese Heart

Astypalaia is often described as a beautiful crossroads where the Cycladic style meets Dodecanese soul, resulting in a uniquely enchanting island. Its iconic whitewashed houses, butterfly-shaped coastline, and serene beaches attract those who want the best of both worlds: stunning Cycladic aesthetics combined with the laid-back hospitality of the Dodecanese.

The Island's Visual Poetry

- The island's Chora (main town) is a picture-perfect Cycladic settlement perched on a hilltop, with winding alleys, whitewashed houses, and vivid blue doors and shutters.
- Castle of Querini: The Venetian castle dominates the skyline, offering breath-taking panoramic views over the Aegean and the island's dramatic coastline.
- The butterfly-shaped island has hidden beaches nestled in coves and open sandy stretches on the windward side.

Beaches & Water sports

- Livadi Beach: A lively, sandy beach near the harbor with cafés and water sports.
- Agios Konstantinos and Kaminakia: Secluded coves ideal for snorkelling and relaxation.
- Windsurfers and sailors are attracted by consistent winds and clear waters.

Traditions & Culture

- Astypalaia's calendar is peppered with festivals honouring saints and local customs, many featuring traditional music and dance.
- The island has a reputation for its local artisan products, including honey, wine, and pottery.
- A blend of Cycladic and Dodecanese influences enriches both the architecture and culinary offerings.

Food & Drink

- Don't miss the fresh seafood, especially octopus and calamari.
- Try "Pitaridia" (traditional savoury pies) and "Ksinomizithra" cheese, a local delicacy.
- The island's wine, produced from indigenous grapes, pairs beautifully with almost any meal.

Ideal For

- Lovers of Cycladic beauty with a twist
- Travelers seeking a peaceful yet lively atmosphere
- Culture and gastronomy enthusiasts

"Astypalaia feels like a hidden jewel, where every corner invites you to pause, breathe, and fall a little deeper in love."

E. Lipsi, Arki & Agathonisi – Secret Islands for True Explorers

For the adventurous few, the small islands of Lipsi, Arki, and Agathonisi represent the ultimate secret escape—a cluster of tranquil, less-visited isles where life moves to the rhythm of the sea and the sun, far from crowds and commercial tourism.

Lipsi – The Hub of the Mini-Archipelago

- Lipsi is the largest and most accessible of the three, with a quaint harbor, traditional whitewashed houses, and a few charming cafés and tavernas.
- The island's natural beauty includes sandy coves like Platis Gialos, ideal for swimming and snorkelling.
- The relaxed atmosphere attracts travelers looking for a quiet but not isolated experience.

Arki – Untouched Beauty

- Arki is even smaller and less developed, known for its crystal-clear waters, secluded beaches, and rugged hiking trails.
- Visitors come here to disconnect and enjoy authentic island life, with a handful of locals maintaining a peaceful pace of life.
- Small guesthouses and family tavernas provide simple but warm hospitality.

Agathonisi – The Quietest Jewel

- Agathonisi is the most remote and least visited, offering unmatched tranquillity.
- Its landscape is dotted with rocky hills, olive groves, and tiny fishing villages.
- Ideal for contemplative travelers who want to fully unplug and enjoy nature's quiet.

What to Expect

- No luxury resorts or bustling nightlife—these islands prioritize simplicity and authenticity.
- Perfect for day trips, slow travel, or as part of an island-hopping itinerary focusing on offbeat paths.

- The local communities are small but deeply welcoming, often inviting visitors to join in communal meals or celebrations.

Ideal For

- True explorers craving solitude and unspoiled nature
- Travelers looking to experience Greek island life at its purest
- Hikers, swimmers, and slow travelers who cherish discovery over convenience

"On these islands, time slows, the sea calms, and the heart opens— an invitation to reconnect with the very essence of travel."

CHAPTER

5

Unforgettable Experiences

Top 10 Must-Do Experiences in the Dodecanese

These handpicked experiences are more than just attractions; they are immersive moments that define the islands and create lifelong memories. Here's what you absolutely cannot miss:

1. Explore the Medieval Old Town of Rhodes

The UNESCO World Heritage-listed Rhodes Old Town is a labyrinth of cobbled streets, towering walls, and vibrant squares. Wander through the Palace of the Grand Master, marvel at Byzantine churches, and soak in the atmosphere where knights once ruled.

- **Tip**: Visit early morning or late afternoon to avoid crowds and enjoy soft golden light.
- **Insider**: Grab a coffee at a café overlooking the harbor after your walk.

2. Climb the Castle of Astypalaia

Perched on a hilltop, this Venetian castle offers panoramic views over the island's butterfly shape and the Aegean Sea. Exploring its ruins and maze-like alleys is a journey back in time, with spectacular photo opportunities.

3. Dive or Snorkel Among Kalymnos' Cliffs

Kalymnos is internationally renowned as a rock climbing paradise, but its underwater world is equally spectacular. Dive into crystal-clear waters to discover colorful reefs, sea caves, and abundant marine life.

- Insider: Join a sponge diving tour to learn about this centuries-old local tradition.

4. Attend the Patmos Easter Festival

One of the most spiritual and moving celebrations in the Greek Orthodox calendar happens on Patmos during Easter. Witness candlelit processions, traditional music, and heartfelt prayers in the very place where the Book of Revelation was written.

5. Sail the Dodecanese Archipelago

A sailing trip is perhaps the best way to appreciate the geography and diversity of the islands. Chart your course to hidden bays, swim off the boat, and enjoy sunsets from the water with nothing but the sea around you.

- Tip: Rent a sailboat or join a group tour from Rhodes or Kos.

6. Hike the Untamed Trails of Karpathos

For adventurous travelers, Karpathos offers rugged mountain trails connecting remote villages. The views of the Aegean below are breath-taking, and the trails are peppered with ancient chapels and traditional stone houses.

7. Discover the Volcanic Wonders of Nisyros

Step into a lunar landscape at the Stefanos Crater, an active volcano with fumaroles and sulphur vents. Guided tours let you explore safely while learning about geology and local myths.

8. Taste Local Flavours at a Village Taverna

Nothing beats sharing a slow, family-style meal in a small village tavern. Taste fresh seafood, homemade cheeses, local honey, and traditional dishes like moussaka or kreatopita (meat pie), paired with a glass of island wine or ouzo.

- Insider: Ask for mezze, a selection of small plates perfect for sharing.

9. Relax on the Sandy Beaches of Kos

Kos offers some of the best beaches in the Dodecanese, perfect for families and sun worshippers alike. The fine sand and shallow waters create safe spots for kids and offer a full day of seaside fun.

10. Experience the Nightlife of Rhodes and Kos Town

After a day of exploration, the towns of Rhodes and Kos light up with bars, clubs, and live music venues. Whether you want to dance until dawn or sip cocktails in a stylish lounge, the islands' nightlife caters to every mood.

Best Beaches by Type

The Dodecanese boasts a stunning variety of beaches to suit every traveller's preference. From family-friendly sands to secret snorkelling coves and dramatic sunset viewpoints, here's an extensive guide to the best beaches categorized by type.

Family-Friendly Beaches

These beaches have calm, shallow waters, facilities, and easy access—perfect for families with kids or those seeking convenience.

- Tigaki Beach, Kos: Long stretches of fine sand and shallow turquoise waters, with sunbeds, tavernas, and water sports.
- Faliraki Beach, Rhodes: Well-organized with playgrounds, cafes, and lifeguards, ideal for a worry-free family day.
- Agathi Beach, Karpathos: A hidden gem with soft sand and gentle waves, less crowded but safe for kids.

Secluded & Quiet Beaches

For travelers seeking tranquillity away from crowds, these beaches offer peaceful escapes surrounded by nature.

- Ladiko Beach, Rhodes: Nestled between rocky coves, ideal for a quiet swim and sunbathing with dramatic cliffs framing the bay.
- Vatses Beach, Kalymnos: Accessible only by boat or hiking trails, this beach rewards effort with pristine waters and solitude.
- Agios Nikolaos, Kasos: A tiny sandy bay with minimal facilities, perfect for those who want raw nature and silence.

Best Beaches for Snorkelling & Diving

The clear waters and diverse marine ecosystems make the Dodecanese a snorkeler's paradise.

- Plati Gialos, Astypalaia: Rocky seabeds and caves provide habitats for colorful fish and octopus.
- Marmari, Kasos: Calm, crystal-clear waters rich with underwater flora and fauna.
- Vroulidia Bay, Patmos: Excellent visibility and interesting underwater rock formations.

Best Beaches for Sunset Viewing

Few things rival watching the sun sink below the horizon with the sea glowing golden. These spots are known for their breath-taking sunsets.

- Haraki Beach, Rhodes: The setting sun paints the sky above the bay with vibrant hues, often enjoyed from beachside tavernas.
- Kamares Bay, Leros: A perfect vantage point with calm waters and a relaxed atmosphere.
- Lipsi Harbor Beach: Watch the sunset behind fishing boats and pastel-coloured houses for a postcard moment.

Bonus Tips for Enjoying the Beaches

- Arrive early to secure the best spots, especially in peak season.
- Bring reef-safe sunscreen to protect both your skin and the fragile marine environment.
- Respect local guidelines and avoid leaving trash behind— the islands' natural beauty depends on responsible tourism.
- Consider renting a beach umbrella and chairs at busier spots for comfort.
- Don't miss the opportunity to try local beach snacks and drinks, like fresh fruit or homemade lemonade.

Whether it's wandering ancient streets, diving beneath the waves, or simply savoring a sunset on a quiet beach, the Dodecanese offers unforgettable experiences for every traveller's soul. These moments—rich with history, nature, and warmth—are the true treasures of the islands.

Historical Sites & Ancient Marvels

The Dodecanese Islands are a living museum, a place where the echoes of ancient civilizations resonate in every stone, ruin, and monument. History here is not just something to observe but to experience—walking through archaeological sites, standing inside ancient temples, and imagining the lives of those who shaped the course of Mediterranean culture. For history enthusiasts and curious travelers alike, the Dodecanese offers a dazzling array of historical treasures that span millennia.

Rhodes: The Medieval and Ancient Powerhouse

Rhodes is undoubtedly the crown jewel of the Dodecanese for lovers of history. The island's Medieval Old Town, one of the best-preserved in Europe, transports you to the era of the Knights of St. John. Massive fortifications, cobblestone streets, and grand palaces stand as testimony to the island's strategic importance during the Crusades.

But Rhodes is not just medieval. The ancient city of Kamiros, one of the three ancient Doric cities on the island, offers fascinating ruins of temples, houses, and marketplaces dating back to the 5th century BC. Nearby, the Acropolis of Lindos crowns a steep cliff, where the remains of a Doric temple dedicated to Athena overlook the sea in breath-taking fashion.

Kos: Cradle of Hippocrates

Kos is famed as the birthplace of Hippocrates, the "Father of Medicine," and the island wears its heritage proudly. The Asklepion, an ancient medical sanctuary dedicated to the god of healing, is a highlight. Wander its ruins where patients once sought cures, and imagine the pioneering medical practices developed here more than two millennia ago.

The island also boasts the Roman Odeon and Agora in Kos Town—stunning archaeological sites with remarkably well-preserved mosaics, columns, and theaters that reveal the richness of urban life in the Roman era.

Patmos: The Island of Revelation

Patmos holds profound spiritual and historical significance as the place where Saint John the Theologian wrote the Book of Revelation. The Cave of the Apocalypse is a pilgrimage site where tradition says the visions were received. Nearby, the Monastery of Saint John stands as a formidable fortress-monastery with a priceless collection of manuscripts and icons, blending history, art, and religion.

Leros, Karpathos & Beyond: Hidden Historical Gems

Leros is dotted with ancient castles and fortresses, including the Castle of Panteli and the Castle of Pandeli, which offer a glimpse into the island's Byzantine and medieval past. On Karpathos, the ancient city ruins of Vrykous invite discovery, offering a remote archaeological site far from the beaten path.

Why History Matters in the Dodecanese

Exploring these sites isn't just about ticking off tourist attractions—it's about connecting with the spirit of the islands. You'll see how the Dodecanese has been a crossroads of civilizations—Greek, Roman, Byzantine, Ottoman, and more—each layer adding depth and character to the landscape.

Monasteries, Castles & Sacred Trails

The spiritual and military architecture of the Dodecanese is a compelling chapter of its heritage, painting a picture of islands that were both battlegrounds and sanctuaries. From rugged castles guarding harbors to monasteries perched on cliffs, these sites offer insights into faith, defense, and the islanders' resilience.

Castles and Fortresses: Guardians of the Sea

- **The Palace of the Grand Master, Rhodes:** This imposing fortress-palace was the seat of the Knights Hospitaller. Its thick walls and towers tell stories of sieges and battles while also showcasing Gothic architecture, a rarity in Greece.
- **The Castle of Monolithos, Rhodes:** Perched atop a steep rock, this ruin offers spectacular views and a haunting atmosphere. It's less visited, perfect for explorers craving solitude amid history.
- **The Castle of Agios Nikolaos, Leros:** A Venetian castle with panoramic views over the sea and the island, a reminder of Leros' strategic importance in naval history.

Monasteries: Islands of Faith and Solitude

- **Monastery of Saint John, Patmos:** Beyond its historical significance, this monastery is an active religious center. Visitors can attend services, admire Byzantine frescoes, and appreciate the tranquil cloisters.
- **Panormitis Monastery, Symi:** Dedicated to the Archangel Michael, it is a spiritual heart of Symi and a pilgrimage site. The monastery's architecture and the surrounding landscape make it a peaceful refuge.
- **Monastery of Profitis Ilias, Rhodes:** Nestled high in the hills, it combines religious devotion with spectacular nature views, ideal for a contemplative visit.

Sacred Trails and Pilgrimages

Several islands feature sacred hiking trails that connect monasteries, chapels, and holy sites, often through breath-taking natural landscapes.

- The Holy Mountain of Mount Profitis Ilias, Rhodes: Hike through pine forests to reach monasteries and chapels with magnificent views.
- Pilgrimage Trail of Patmos: Connects the Cave of the Apocalypse to various sacred spots across the island, blending spirituality with exercise.

These trails invite visitors to combine physical activity with cultural and spiritual discovery—a holistic experience that resonates deeply.

Experiencing the Sacred

Visiting these sites often means experiencing local religious festivals and traditions. Many monasteries celebrate feast days with processions, music, and communal feasts, giving visitors a chance to engage with islanders beyond sightseeing.

Water sports: Diving, Windsurfing, Snorkelling & More

The Dodecanese's turquoise waters and varied coastal conditions make it a prime destination for water sports enthusiasts. Whether you crave the adrenaline of windsurfing, the serenity of snorkelling over reefs, or the thrill of deep diving, the islands offer a spectrum of aquatic adventures that showcase the vibrant marine ecosystem and breath-taking seascapes.

Diving: Underwater Wonders

The islands of Kalymnos, Rhodes, and Kasos are especially famous for diving. Kalymnos, known as the "Island of Sponges," has dive sites rich in underwater caves, reefs, and historic shipwrecks.

- **Kalymnos Diving:** Dive centers offer courses and guided dives for all levels. Explore sites like the Sponge Docks, or venture to deeper wrecks for advanced divers.
- **Rhodes Diving:** From shallow reefs to dramatic drop-offs, Rhodes offers diverse dive experiences. The Kalimnos Wreck is a popular dive spot teeming with fish.
- **Kasos Diving:** Known for its crystal-clear waters and less crowded dive sites, it's ideal for those seeking pristine underwater visibility.

Windsurfing and Kiteboarding

The Aegean winds provide perfect conditions for windsurfing and kiteboarding, especially on islands like Rhodes and Kos.

- Prasonisi Beach, Rhodes: Often called the windsurfing capital of the Dodecanese, it offers both flat water lagoons and wave-riding zones, suitable for beginners and pros alike.
- Tigaki Beach, Kos: Known for steady winds and warm waters, this is a hotspot for windsurfing schools and equipment rentals.

Snorkelling: Discovering Shallow Marine Life

Snorkelling here is a vibrant experience, with many bays featuring rocky seabeds and abundant fish species.

- Vroulidia Bay, Patmos: Clear, calm waters perfect for spotting colorful fish and sea urchins.

- Marmari Bay, Kasos: Excellent visibility and interesting rock formations invite exploration just below the surface.
- Agios Nikolaos, Rhodes: Quiet coves with shallow waters ideal for family snorkelling.

Kayaking, Paddle boarding & Sailing

For those who prefer to explore above water, the calm bays and sheltered coastlines are perfect for kayaking and paddle boarding.

- Rent a kayak to paddle around Symi's spectacular harbors or explore hidden coves only accessible by water.
- Sailing trips offer the best way to island-hop and access secluded beaches, with options from private charters to group excursions.

Practical Tips for Water sports

- Safety First: Always check weather and sea conditions, especially if you're new to any water sport.
- Local Schools and Rentals: Most popular islands have certified instructors and rental shops, offering lessons for beginners and equipment for experienced enthusiasts.
- Respect Marine Life: Use reef-safe sunscreens, avoid touching coral or disturbing wildlife, and follow local regulations.

Why Water Sports Matter in the Dodecanese

The Dodecanese's waters are an integral part of the island experience. Engaging in water sports not only adds excitement and variety to your trip but also connects you to the natural environment in an intimate way. Whether you're drifting above coral reefs, slicing through waves on a windsurfing board, or paddling into a secluded bay, the sea here invites exploration and discovery.

Sailing & Island-Hopping Day Trips

Sailing the shimmering Aegean waters around the Dodecanese is not just a mode of transport—it's a quintessential part of the island experience. The Dodecanese archipelago, with its more than 150 islands and islets, offers an unparalleled playground for sailors, both seasoned and novice. From luxury yachts and private charters to traditional caiques and public ferries, island-hopping here is a thrilling adventure and an intimate way to discover hidden gems that are unreachable by land.

Why Sail the Dodecanese?

The islands' close proximity to each other makes sailing an ideal way to explore multiple destinations in a single day. You can wake up in the medieval streets of Rhodes, spend the afternoon swimming in crystal-clear coves on Symi, and enjoy dinner in a seaside taverna on Kos—all in one day.

The ever-present Aegean winds and generally calm seas from spring to early autumn provide excellent sailing conditions. Plus, sailing routes allow you to bypass crowded tourist hotspots, revealing secret beaches, quiet fishing villages, and secluded bays.

Popular Island-Hopping Routes

- Rhodes – Symi – Halki: A classic route starting from Rhodes, heading to the glamour of Symi with its pastel neoclassical harbor, and then to the tranquil, car-free island of Halki for authentic Greek island vibes.
- Kos – Nisyros – Tilos: Begin in Kos and sail to Nisyros, famous for its volcanic caldera and steaming fumaroles, then onward to eco-conscious Tilos with its wild landscapes and nature reserves.

- Karpathos – Kasos – Astypalaia: For adventurous travelers, this less trodden route connects islands with dramatic landscapes, from the rugged mountains of Karpathos to the raw simplicity of Kasos and the Cycladic charm of Astypalaia.

Day Trips vs. Extended Sailing

Day trips on traditional boats and motor yachts are available from most main islands and are a popular way to sample the sailing lifestyle without the commitment. These trips often include stops for swimming, snorkelling, and seaside lunches, and are great for families or travelers short on time.

For a deeper experience, consider renting a sailing yacht for several days. Whether you hire a skipper or charter bareboat, sailing yourself allows you to customize your itinerary, linger in your favourite spots, and explore off-the-beaten-path islands.

What to Expect on a Sailing Trip

- **Sunrise and Sunset at Sea:** There's nothing like the serenity of sailing at dawn or watching the sun dip behind an island horizon, painting the sky in pink and gold hues.
- **Swimming in Secluded Bays:** Many islands have hidden coves accessible only by boat, where you can swim in turquoise waters far from crowds.
- **Traditional Cuisine on Board or on Shore:** Most sailing excursions include fresh seafood lunches, often featuring locally sourced ingredients, or stop at waterfront tavernas.
- **Friendly Island Hospitality:** Each island's harbor is welcoming, and locals are often happy to share stories or recommend hidden spots.

Sailing Tips for Visitors

- Book in advance during the high season (July-August) as charters and day trips fill up quickly.
- If you're sailing yourself, ensure you understand local maritime regulations and weather patterns.
- Pack light, bring sun protection, a hat, and water shoes for rocky landings.
- Respect marine protected areas and wildlife by sailing responsibly.

Hiking & Nature Trails by Island

The Dodecanese isn't just about sun and sea—it's a paradise for hikers and nature lovers. The islands' diverse landscapes offer an extensive network of trails, from easy coastal walks to challenging mountain routes. Hiking here is more than exercise; it's a way to connect deeply with the land, discover hidden villages, ancient ruins, and panoramic vistas that few tourists ever see.

Rhodes: Trails Through History and Nature

- Profitis Ilias Mountain: Rhodes' highest peak features several trails winding through pine forests and past monasteries. The summit offers sweeping views of the island and sea.
- The Valley of the Butterflies (Petaloudes): A unique natural reserve where thousands of Jersey tiger moths gather in summer. Walking paths wind through shaded groves and streams.
- Ancient Kamiros Trail: Hike among olive groves and ruins with breath-taking views of the west coast and the Aegean.

Kos: From Thermal Springs to Volcanic Hills

- Dikeos Mountain: The highest point on Kos offers challenging hikes through fragrant pine and cypress forests, culminating in stunning views over the island.
- Asklepion to Zia Village: This trail passes through olive groves and traditional villages, perfect for a day hike with cultural stops.
- Thermal Springs Walks: Explore paths around natural springs known for their healing properties.

Symi, Chalki & Smaller Islands: Coastal Walks and Pastoral Trails

- Symi's Marathounda to Pedi Beach: A scenic coastal hike past hidden bays, traditional chapels, and rocky coves.
- Chalki's Venetian Castle Trail: A gentle walk leading to the island's castle ruins with views of the Aegean's pastel palette.

Kalymnos & Karpathos: For the Adventurous

- Kalymnos Rock Climbing Trails: While famous for climbing, Kalymnos also offers hiking paths through terraced fields, sponge-diving villages, and secluded beaches.
- Karpathos' Mt. Kali Limni to Olympos Village: This rugged trail leads to one of the island's most isolated and culturally rich villages, preserving traditional customs and dialect.

Tilos and Nisyros: Eco-Trails

- Tilos Natura 2000 Trails: Eco-conscious trails lead through protected habitats with endemic plants and rare bird species.

- Nisyros Volcano Hike: Walk into the heart of an active volcanic crater, feeling the steam vents and witnessing a unique geological landscape.

Why Hiking Matters in the Dodecanese

Hiking reveals the islands' hidden layers—terraced hillsides, ancient footpaths, and panoramic views—providing a refreshing counterpoint to beach days. It offers a chance to move at a slower pace, engage with local nature, and gain a new perspective on island life.

Photography Spots & Instagram-Worthy Views

The Dodecanese Islands are a dream for photographers, whether professional or casual. Their dramatic landscapes, vibrant villages, historic sites, and sparkling seas combine into a visual feast. Every island has its iconic spots that have graced countless social media feeds, but beyond those, there are countless hidden gems that reward exploration and an eye for beauty.

Rhodes: Medieval Charm Meets Coastal Splendour

- Rhodes Old Town Gateways: The stone arches and cobbled streets create perfect frames for moody, historic shots.
- Lindos Acropolis at Sunset: Capture the ancient temple ruins glowing with golden light, set against the Aegean.
- Elli Beach Pier: The contrast between deep blue waters and sunbathers makes for vibrant summer shots.

Kos: Bright Colors and Timeless Ruins

- Hippocrates Plane Tree, Kos Town: The ancient tree and surrounding cafes offer a charming mix of nature and culture.
- Asklepion Ruins at Dawn: Misty mornings here create atmospheric images of pillars and stonework.
- Marmari Bay: Turquoise water and white pebbled beaches perfect for minimalistic nature shots.

Symi: Pastel Harbors and Neoclassical Elegance

- Gialos Harbor: The pastel-coloured neoclassical buildings reflected on the calm harbor water make an Instagram staple.
- Ano Symi Village: Narrow streets with brightly painted doors and flower pots provide perfect portraits of traditional island life.

Karpathos and Kalymnos: Rugged and Raw

- Olympos Village, Karpathos: Traditional costumes, stone houses, and wild landscapes combine for authentic cultural photography.
- Kalymnos Cliffs: Dramatic rocky coastlines and colorful fishing boats offer dynamic shots.

Nisyros Volcano & Tilos' Natural Wonders

- Volcanic Crater Rim, Nisyros: Steam vents and lunar-like terrain give an otherworldly feel.
- Tilos Beaches at Golden Hour: Soft, warm light enhances the natural colors and tranquillity.

Tips for Capturing the Dodecanese

- Golden Hours: Early mornings and late afternoons provide the best light, softer shadows, and stunning colors.
- Respect Privacy and Sacred Spaces: Always ask permission before photographing locals or entering sacred areas.
- Bring Variety: A wide-angle lens for landscapes, a zoom for wildlife or distant details, and a good smartphone camera for quick shots.
- Explore Beyond the Hotspots: Some of the best photos come from wandering off main roads and discovering small chapels, fishing villages, and quiet coves.

Why Photography Enhances Your Trip

Capturing the beauty of the Dodecanese allows you to relive memories and share the magic with friends and family. Photography encourages you to slow down, observe details, and appreciate the layers of history, culture, and nature that make these islands unforgettable.

CHAPTER

6

Food, Culture & Island Life

Introduction to Dodecanese Cuisine

The Dodecanese Islands, nestled in the south eastern Aegean Sea, offer not only breath-taking landscapes but also a rich culinary tapestry that reflects centuries of history, cultural fusion, and the bounty of both land and sea. Exploring the food of the Dodecanese is an essential part of any visit—more than just nourishment, it's a vibrant expression of island life, tradition, and hospitality.

The cuisine here is deeply rooted in Mediterranean principles: fresh, seasonal, and local ingredients prepared with simplicity and respect. The islands' geographical position, close to Asia Minor, North Africa, and mainland Greece, means that Dodecanese cooking is a fascinating melting pot where Greek, Turkish, Italian, and Middle Eastern influences mingle seamlessly. The result is a unique palette of flavours, textures, and aromas that tell stories of trade, migration, and resilience.

Key Ingredients and Flavours

- **Olive Oil:** Often called "liquid gold," olive oil is the cornerstone of Dodecanese cooking. Many families produce their own oil, and it's generously used for cooking, dressing salads, and drizzling over fresh bread.
- **Fresh Seafood:** Surrounded by the Aegean's crystal-clear waters, the islands offer a daily catch of octopus, squid, grouper, sea bass, and the prized red mullet. Freshness is paramount, and seafood often finds its way simply grilled or baked.
- **Herbs and Aromatics:** Wild herbs like oregano, thyme, rosemary, and mint grow abundantly. Island cooks use these herbs liberally, enhancing dishes with distinct aromatic notes that evoke the Mediterranean landscape.
- **Vegetables and Legumes:** Seasonal produce—eggplants, tomatoes, zucchini, green beans, and fava beans—feature

prominently, often slow-cooked in olive oil with garlic and onions. Legumes like chickpeas and lentils provide hearty protein, especially in traditional stews.

- Cheeses: Local cheeses such as Petimezi (a sweet grape molasses) and Kefalotyri (a hard sheep's milk cheese) add flavour and texture to many dishes, often served grilled or as part of salads.

Eating as a Social and Cultural Experience

In the Dodecanese, food is never rushed. Meals are social events where family and friends gather, stories are shared, and traditions are passed down. The leisurely mezze culture—plates of small dishes shared communally—is perfect for savoring variety and encourages lingering conversation.

Tavernas, family-run and humble, are the beating heart of local food culture. You'll find locals gathered over glasses of retsina or ouzo, enjoying hearty plates of grilled meats or seafood, homemade bread, and seasonal vegetables. Many tavernas have menus that change daily, reflecting what's fresh and available that morning at market or sea.

Festivals and Food Traditions

Food is central to the islands' vibrant festivals and religious celebrations. For instance, during Easter, families prepare magiritsa, a traditional lamb offal soup served at midnight, while Christmas brings melomakarona (honey-soaked cookies) and kourabiedes (almond shortbread).

Harvest festivals celebrate the olive crop and grape harvest, with feasts that include freshly pressed olive oil tastings and homemade wine. These communal events are excellent opportunities for visitors to dive into authentic island life and cuisine.

Modern Influences and Culinary Innovation

While traditional cooking remains alive and well, the Dodecanese also embraces contemporary culinary trends. Upscale restaurants in Rhodes and Kos have garnered acclaim for creatively fusing local ingredients with international techniques, offering gourmet interpretations of classic dishes. Organic farming and farm-to-table concepts are growing, as younger chefs bring innovation while respecting heritage.

Whether dining in a rustic village taverna or a chic seaside bistro, the essence of Dodecanese cuisine—freshness, hospitality, and deep connection to the land and sea—shines through.

Must-Try Dishes, Desserts & Drinks

The true taste of the Dodecanese comes alive in its iconic dishes, sweets, and beverages. Sampling these specialties will deepen your appreciation of the islands' culinary heritage and make your visit unforgettable.

Must-Try Dishes

- **Pitaroudia**: These golden, crispy chickpea fritters, seasoned with herbs and garlic, are a local favourite appetizer or snack. Perfect with a squeeze of lemon and a side of tzatziki.
- **Krasotiri Cheese Pie:** A savoury pie made with local kefalotyri cheese and a splash of island wine, wrapped in flaky phyllo dough. It's a comforting, rustic dish often found in village bakeries.
- **Keftedes (Meatballs):** Unlike mainland versions, Dodecanese keftedes often include herbs like mint and oregano, creating a fragrant and moist bite. They're usually served with tzatziki or tomato sauce.

- **Octopus Stifado:** A slow-cooked stew of octopus in red wine with onions, tomatoes, and cinnamon—a rich and tender dish that encapsulates the sea's bounty and the island's love of robust flavours.
- **Moussaka Dodecanese Style:** Layers of eggplant, minced meat, potatoes, and béchamel sauce, baked to golden perfection. The local version often incorporates unique spice blends giving it a distinct taste.
- **Lahanosalata**: A cabbage salad tossed with olive oil, vinegar, and sometimes fresh herbs, served as a refreshing side that cuts through richer dishes.

Delectable Desserts

- **Soumada**: A traditional almond syrup drink served especially during festivals. It's sweet, aromatic, and deeply rooted in island culture.
- **Kadaifi**: A dessert of shredded phyllo dough soaked in honey syrup and layered with nuts—crispy on the outside, sweet and sticky within.
- **Baklava**: The classic Greek sweet of layered filo pastry, nuts, and syrup, but in the Dodecanese, it often features local almonds or walnuts, making it slightly different from other regions.
- **Amygdalota**: Soft almond cookies, lightly scented with rose or orange blossom water, offering a delicate sweetness that pairs perfectly with coffee.
- **Mastelo**: A traditional sweet cheese dessert from Karpathos, made from fresh goat cheese and honey, often baked in a clay pot—a rare treat that reflects local cheese-making traditions.

Traditional Drinks

- **Ouzo**: The iconic anise-flavoured spirit of Greece, widely enjoyed in the Dodecanese. Sipped slowly, often accompanied by meze, it's a symbol of conviviality.
- **Raki**: A potent grape-based spirit with a strong local following, often homemade and shared generously among friends.
- **Local Wines:** The islands produce unique wines, especially dry reds and aromatic whites. Rhodes is particularly famous for its vineyards, with some varieties dating back to antiquity.
- **Herbal Teas:** Infusions made from wild island herbs such as sage, thyme, and mountain tea are popular for their soothing properties and enjoyed any time of day.

Where to Taste Authentic Flavours

To truly savour Dodecanese cuisine, seek out family-run tavernas away from tourist centers, where recipes have been passed down generations. Village festivals are also perfect for sampling homemade specialties in lively, communal settings.

Farmers' markets bursting with fresh produce, fish markets displaying the day's catch, and bakeries with warm phyllo pies all invite you to engage with the food culture directly.

Eating in the Dodecanese is more than a culinary adventure—it's a journey into the islands' soul. Each bite carries stories of the sea, the soil, the seasons, and the generations who cultivated this rich food heritage. Whether you're savoring a simple grilled fish by the harbor or indulging in a honey-soaked dessert in a mountain village, you'll feel connected to a timeless way of life that celebrates flavour, community, and place.

Dining Guide: Tavernas, Ouzeries, Street Food & Gourmet

The Dodecanese dining scene is a vibrant mosaic, reflecting the islands' rich history, diverse influences, and deep-rooted culinary traditions. Whether you're craving the rustic charm of a family-run taverna, the lively atmosphere of an ouzeri, the quick satisfaction of street food, or the elegance of a gourmet restaurant, the islands have it all—and then some. Understanding where to go and what to expect can transform every meal into a memorable experience.

Tavernas: Heart and Soul of Island Dining

Tavernas are the beating heart of the Dodecanese's culinary culture. These family-owned eateries, often tucked away on narrow alleys or overlooking picturesque harbors, serve up traditional dishes with warm hospitality. Expect simple yet expertly prepared fare, heavy on fresh, local ingredients. Meals here are slow, social affairs designed to be savored.

- **What to Expect:** Menus change daily based on the freshest catch and seasonal produce. You'll find classics like grilled octopus, slow-cooked lamb with herbs, fresh salads dressed with local olive oil, and homemade pies.
- **Atmosphere**: Taverns are lively and unpretentious, buzzing with locals and tourists alike. The clinking of glasses, spirited conversations, and traditional Greek music often create an immersive cultural experience.
- **Tips**: Look for places packed with locals, a sure sign of authenticity. Don't hesitate to ask for the "specials" of the day and pair your meal with a local wine or ouzo.

Ouzeries: Celebrating the Anise Spirit

Ouzeries specialize in ouzo, the quintessential Greek anise-flavoured spirit, and offer a distinct, convivial dining experience. Here, meze plates—small, shared dishes—take center stage, providing a diverse taste of island flavors.

- **Typical Meze:** Think olives, tzatziki, grilled sardines, fried calamari, cheese pies, and spicy sausages. The small portions encourage sampling a variety of tastes in one sitting.
- **Experience**: Ouzeries are casual and social, often bustling with locals enjoying late evenings. They're perfect for a light dinner or a long night of drinking and conversation.
- **Best Spots:** Ouzeries by the water, especially in Rhodes and Kos, offer a fantastic blend of food, drink, and sea views.

Street Food: Quick, Flavourful & Authentic

For those who want to experience the Dodecanese on the go or dive into local flavors without a sit-down meal, street food is a fantastic option. Across the islands, vibrant street food stalls and markets serve up fresh, satisfying bites that reflect both tradition and innovation.

- **Popular Choices:** Gyros and souvlaki—grilled meat wrapped in pita with tomatoes, onions, and tzatziki—are widely beloved. You'll also find cheese-filled pastries, savoury pies, and freshly baked bread with dips.
- **Seasonal Treats:** In summer months, vendors sell cooling treats like loukoumades (honey-soaked doughnuts) and fresh fruit juices.
- **Where to Find:** Town centers, market squares, and harbors buzz with street food vendors, especially in the evenings.

Gourmet Dining: Elevating Tradition

In recent years, the Dodecanese has seen a rise in gourmet dining that artfully elevates traditional recipes with modern techniques and presentation. Upscale restaurants, particularly in Rhodes and Kos, offer innovative tasting menus, farm-to-table concepts, and creative use of local ingredients.

- Cuisine Style: Expect a fusion of Mediterranean flavors with international culinary artistry—think octopus carpaccio, lamb sous-vide with island herbs, or desserts infused with local honey and herbs.
- Wine Pairing: Many gourmet venues boast extensive local wine lists, pairing each course with thoughtfully selected bottles to highlight island vineyards.
- Ambience: Stylish settings, often with sea views or historic surroundings, create a luxurious yet authentic dining experience ideal for special occasions or food enthusiasts.

Wineries, Distilleries & Farm Visits

The Dodecanese islands are not only a feast for the palate but also a destination where visitors can immerse themselves in the art of traditional food and drink production. Exploring local wineries, distilleries, and farms offers a behind-the-scenes look at how the islands' prized products are made and an opportunity to taste them fresh from the source.

Wineries: A Legacy of Ancient Vineyards

The islands of Rhodes, Kos, and Karpathos have a winemaking heritage that dates back thousands of years, with some vineyards tracing their roots to antiquity. Today, boutique wineries blend time-honoured traditions with modern techniques, producing exceptional wines with distinctive island character.

- **Wine Varieties:** Expect robust reds made from indigenous grapes like Athiri and Mandilaria, crisp whites with citrus and floral notes, and sweet dessert wines crafted from sun-dried grapes.
- **Tours and Tastings:** Many wineries offer guided tours where you can wander through vineyards, learn about grape cultivation, and visit cellars. Tastings often include several varieties paired with local cheeses and breads.
- **Recommended Wineries:** The vineyards of Rhodes are especially renowned, with several family-run estates open to visitors for tastings and lunches.

Distilleries: Spirits of the Islands

Distilleries, both traditional and modern, craft ouzo, raki, and other spirits unique to the Dodecanese. Visiting these sites gives insight into the distillation process and the cultural importance of these beverages.

- **Ouzo and Raki:** Learn how these anise-flavoured and grape-based spirits are made, from fermentation to distillation. Many distilleries offer tastings paired with meze and local snacks.
- **Specialty Spirits:** Some islands produce unique liqueurs infused with local herbs and fruits, offering a taste unlike anywhere else.
- **Distillery Experiences:** Small-scale producers often welcome visitors for tours, storytelling, and immersive tastings that bring island traditions to life.

Farm Visits: Taste the Land

Agriculture remains a vital part of island life. Olive groves, herb gardens, and small-scale farms produce many ingredients found on local menus.

- **Olive Oil Farms:** Some farms open their gates for tours showing olive pressing and oil tasting—an unforgettable experience that highlights why island olive oil is so prized.
- **Herb Gardens:** Visit fragrant gardens to discover the wild herbs that flavour so many Dodecanese dishes. You can often sample herbal teas and purchase dried herbs to bring home.
- **Cheese Producers:** Small dairies offer tastings of traditional cheeses, often accompanied by stories of local farming families and their artisanal methods.
- **Farm-to-Table:** Some farms collaborate with local restaurants to supply fresh, organic ingredients, and some offer cooking workshops or meals on-site.

Cultural Events & Festivals

The Dodecanese islands are alive with cultural celebrations year-round. These festivals offer visitors a chance to experience island traditions, music, dance, and food in their most authentic forms. In 2025, the calendar is especially rich with events that celebrate heritage and community spirit, blending ancient customs with modern festivity.

Religious and Traditional Festivals

Religious celebrations are deeply woven into island life, often marking saints' feast days with processions, church services, and communal feasts.

- Easter in the Dodecanese: Easter is the most significant celebration, featuring midnight masses, candlelit processions, and a festive atmosphere that lasts for days. The breaking of the red-dyed eggs and feasting on lamb and local sweets are highlights.
- Feast of Saint John (June 24th): Marked by bonfires and music, this festival celebrates midsummer with traditional dancing and community gatherings.
- Virgin Mary's Assumption (August 15th): Major festivities across islands with religious ceremonies, fireworks, and concerts. Many islanders return home, making it a vibrant time for local culture.

Music, Dance & Arts Festivals

The islands host numerous cultural events showcasing traditional music, dance, and contemporary arts.

- **Rhodes Medieval Festival:** A highlight of the year, this event recreates the medieval era with parades, theatrical performances, medieval markets, and traditional music and dance in the atmospheric Old Town.
- **Kos International Festival:** Featuring concerts, theater, and dance performances, this festival attracts international artists alongside local talent.
- **Local Folk Dances:** Many islands hold regular performances of traditional dances, often open to visitors who want to participate and learn.

Food & Wine Festivals

Celebrate the islands' culinary heritage with festivals dedicated to wine, olives, and local produce.

- **Olive Harvest Festival:** Held in autumn, this festival marks the start of the olive picking season with tastings, traditional music, and communal meals.
- **Wine Festivals:** Rhodes and Kos host annual wine festivals featuring tastings, vineyard tours, and food pairings showcasing the best of local production.

Special Events

- **Dodecanese Gastronomy Week:** A new initiative bringing together chefs, farmers, and producers to celebrate island cuisine through workshops, tastings, and special menus.
- **Maritime Heritage Celebrations:** Several islands will host events honouring their seafaring past, including boat parades and historical exhibitions.
- **Eco-Tourism Days:** Promoting sustainable tourism and conservation, these events include guided hikes, beach clean-ups, and educational talks.

Why Attend?

Participating in festivals and cultural events is one of the most rewarding ways to connect with the Dodecanese spirit. Beyond sightseeing, you'll be welcomed into lively communities where traditions are alive, where the past and present mingle, and where food, music, and dance create memories that last long after you leave the islands.

Artisan Crafts, Markets & Souvenir Ideas

The Dodecanese islands are a treasure trove for lovers of artisan crafts and unique souvenirs, where traditional skills have been lovingly preserved and passed down through generations. Whether you're wandering vibrant local markets, exploring quaint village workshops, or hunting for that perfect keepsake, the islands offer a rich tapestry of handmade goods that reflect their history, culture, and natural beauty.

Artisan Crafts: A Legacy of Skill and Creativity

From Rhodes to the smallest islets, artisan crafts tell the story of the islands' diverse cultural influences and deep respect for tradition. Many craftspeople still use time-honoured techniques combined with locally sourced materials, creating one-of-a-kind items you won't find anywhere else.

- **Ceramics and Pottery:** Handmade pottery, often adorned with traditional geometric patterns and vibrant colors, is a common sight. On Rhodes and Kos, potters shape everything from decorative plates to functional pitchers, each piece reflecting local styles.
- **Textiles and Embroidery:** The Dodecanese have a rich heritage in textile arts, particularly in the form of intricate embroidery. You'll find beautiful table linens, cushion covers, and traditional costumes featuring colorful, detailed needlework in island markets and specialty shops.
- **Jewelry:** Artisans create delicate silver and gold jewelry inspired by ancient Greek motifs, incorporating local stones and pearls. Unique pieces often blend modern design with traditional symbolism, perfect for meaningful gifts.
- **Woodwork and Leather:** From hand-carved wooden icons and furniture to soft leather sandals and bags, the islands offer a range of durable, handcrafted goods made to last.

Markets: Where Culture Meets Commerce

Local markets are the beating heart of island commerce and social life. Here, you can browse fresh produce alongside artisanal crafts, chatting with vendors who are often the very creators of the items on sale.

- **Rhodes Old Town Market:** A vibrant maze of stalls selling everything from spices and herbs to handmade soaps and jewelry. The lively atmosphere and colorful displays make it an unmissable shopping experience.
- **Kos Market Square:** On market days, this central square transforms into a bustling hub of local products, including pottery, textiles, and fresh foods.
- **Village Fairs:** Smaller islands like Leros and Symi host weekly or seasonal fairs where locals gather to sell homemade jams, cheeses, herbs, and crafts, often accompanied by live music and dance.

Souvenir Ideas: Meaningful Mementos

When choosing souvenirs, think beyond the typical trinkets and opt for items that truly capture the spirit of the Dodecanese:

- **Local Olive Oil:** Many island olive oils are award-winning, rich in flavour, and beautifully packaged—perfect for gifting or savoring at home.
- **Herbal Teas and Spices:** Dried herbs like oregano, thyme, and mountain tea are widely used in island cooking and make aromatic, authentic souvenirs.
- **Handmade Soaps and Cosmetics:** Often made from local olive oil and infused with herbs and flowers, these natural products are a fragrant reminder of the islands.
- **Traditional Musical Instruments:** Small bouzoukis or lyres crafted by local artisans can be a special keepsake for music lovers.

Local Customs, Etiquette & Island Traditions

Traveling to the Dodecanese offers more than stunning views—it's an immersion into a culture shaped by centuries of history, religion, and community. Understanding local customs and etiquette enriches your experience and helps you connect respectfully and genuinely with islanders.

Welcoming Hospitality

Hospitality is a cornerstone of Greek island life. Islanders often greet visitors warmly, sometimes inviting them to share a coffee, ouzo, or homemade treat. Accepting these gestures is a way to build bonds and experience the islands beyond the surface.

- Greetings: A friendly "Kalimera" (Good morning) or "Kalispera" (Good evening) goes a long way. Handshakes are common, and among closer acquaintances, cheek kisses (usually twice) are the norm.
- Invitations: If invited to a local's home, bringing a small gift such as sweets, wine, or flowers is appreciated.

Dress and Behavior

While the islands are generally relaxed, modest dress is respectful, especially when visiting religious sites.

- **Church Visits:** Cover shoulders and knees when entering churches and monasteries. Speaking softly and switching phones to silent are expected.
- **Public Conduct:** Greeks are expressive and social, but public displays of affection are usually modest. Loud or boisterous behavior is generally frowned upon.

Dining Etiquette

Sharing food is a ritual that symbolizes friendship and community. Meals can last hours, with plenty of conversation and multiple courses.

- **Sharing**: Expect dishes to be shared family-style. It's polite to try a bit of everything offered.
- **Punctuality**: Don't stress about strict timing; island life runs at its own relaxed pace, but showing up too early or late can be impolite.
- **Toasting**: When toasting with ouzo or wine, maintaining eye contact is important. Saying "Yamas" (Cheers) is a good way to join in.

Festivals and Celebrations

Participating respectfully in local festivals is a highlight for many visitors. Observe how islanders dress, celebrate, and interact, and follow their lead in participation.

- **Photography**: Always ask permission before taking close-up photos of people, especially during religious events.
- **Gifts and Offerings:** In some festivals, it's customary to bring small donations or gifts to churches or community events.

Language Guide: Key Greek Phrases for Travelers

While English is widely spoken in tourist areas, knowing basic Greek phrases enhances your interaction with locals and shows respect for their culture. Many islanders appreciate even a modest effort to speak their language, and it often opens doors to richer experiences.

Greetings & Polite Expressions

- Kalimera (καλημέρα) — Good morning
- Kalispera (καλησπέρα) — Good evening
- Kalinikhta (καληνύχτα) — Good night
- Efharisto (ευχαριστώ) — Thank you
- Parakalo (παρακαλώ) — Please / You're welcome
- Signomi (συγγνώμη) — Excuse me / Sorry
- Nai / Ohi (ναι / όχι) — Yes / No

Travel Essentials

- Pou ine…? (Πού είναι…;) — Where is…?
- Poso kanei? (Πόσο κάνει;) — How much does it cost?
- To lefko krasi, parakalo. (Το λευκό κρασί, παρακαλώ.) — White wine, please.
- Eho alergia. (Έχω αλλεργία.) — I have an allergy.
- Tha ithela ena trapezi gia dyo. (Θα ήθελα ένα τραπέζι για δύο.) — I would like a table for two.

Numbers

- Ena, Dyo, Tria, Tessera, Pente — One, Two, Three, Four, Five
- Deka, Eikosi, Trianta — Ten, Twenty, Thirty

Knowing these can help with prices, directions, and quantities.

Useful Phrases for Island Life

- To neró, parakaló. (Το νερό, παρακαλώ.) — Water, please.
- I piátsa tou leofórou. (Η πιάτσα του λεωφορείου.) — The bus station.
- Ypóhoresí me lámi. (Υποχρέωση με λάμψη.) — Emergency with a phone call.

- Eínai pántes agapitoí. (Είναι πάντες αγαπητοί.) — Everyone is kind.

Pronunciation Tips

Greek is phonetic, so words are pronounced as they are written. Stress usually falls on the penultimate syllable. For example, "Kaliméra" sounds like "kah-lee-MEH-rah."

Mastering even a few phrases helps break the ice and enriches your interactions, making your Dodecanese journey more immersive and memorable.

CHAPTER

7

Tailored Itineraries

The Dodecanese archipelago, with its mosaic of islands, offers a wealth of experiences—historic towns, pristine beaches, dramatic landscapes, and vibrant local culture. Whether you're visiting for a quick escape or a longer expedition, having a carefully crafted itinerary can make all the difference between a rushed trip and a deeply rewarding adventure. Below are two tailored itineraries designed to suit different traveller types and schedules, ensuring you get the most from your Dodecanese journey.

5-Day Essentials Tour (Easy Highlights for First-Timers)

Perfect for travelers visiting the Dodecanese for the first time or those with limited time, this itinerary focuses on must-see highlights, blending culture, relaxation, and scenic exploration without feeling overwhelming. It strikes a gentle pace, offering a taste of the islands' rich history and natural beauty.

Day 1: Rhodes – Medieval Magic & Local Flavour

- **Morning**: Arrive in Rhodes, the largest and most accessible island. Head straight to the UNESCO-listed Medieval Old Town, one of Europe's best-preserved walled cities. Wander the cobblestone streets, exploring the Palace of the Grand Master and the Street of the Knights.
- **Lunch**: Dine at a traditional taverna inside the Old Town, trying local specialties like *melekouni* (sesame honey bars) and fresh seafood.
- **Afternoon**: Visit the Archaeological Museum housed in the medieval Hospital of the Knights to get an overview of Rhodes' rich history.
- **Evening**: Stroll along the Mandraki Harbor, enjoy sunset views, and sip an ouzo at a waterfront café.

Day 2: Rhodes Beaches & Ancient Lindos

- **Morning**: Take a morning trip to Lindos, a picturesque village known for its clifftop Acropolis with panoramic Aegean views. Climb or take a donkey ride up, explore ancient ruins, and wander whitewashed alleys.
- **Lunch**: Enjoy fresh grilled fish at a seaside taverna in Lindos Bay.
- **Afternoon**: Relax on St. Paul's Bay beach or Tsambika Beach, ideal for swimming and sunbathing.
- **Evening**: Return to Rhodes town for a relaxed dinner and perhaps a cultural show.

Day 3: Kos – Healing History & Vibrant Nightlife

- **Morning**: Take an early ferry (approx. 1 hour) to Kos. Begin your day at the Asklepion, an ancient healing temple and medical center that's one of the most important archaeological sites in the Dodecanese.
- **Lunch**: Sample *pitaroudia* (chickpea fritters) at a local eatery.
- **Afternoon**: Explore Kos Town's Venetian Castle and bustling market streets, perfect for shopping souvenirs and people-watching.
- **Evening**: Experience Kos' vibrant nightlife with seaside bars and music.

Day 4: Patmos – Spiritual and Serene

- **Morning**: Ferry to Patmos (approx. 1.5-2 hours). Visit the Monastery of Saint John the Theologian and the nearby Cave of the Apocalypse, where the Book of Revelation was said to be written.
- **Lunch**: Taste fresh island specialties like *astakomakaronada* (lobster pasta) at a waterfront restaurant.

- **Afternoon**: Wander through Chora, a fortified village with narrow alleys and stunning sea views.
- **Evening**: Enjoy a peaceful sunset at Psili Ammos Beach.

Day 5: Relaxation & Departure

- **Morning**: Take a leisurely morning walk or swim at one of the local beaches.
- **Midday**: Return to Rhodes by ferry or flight for your departure, with enough time to pick up last-minute souvenirs or enjoy a final meal in town.

Why this works for first-timers:

This itinerary balances iconic sites with relaxation, pacing your days to avoid travel fatigue. It provides a well-rounded experience of the Dodecanese's history, culture, and nature, perfect for discovering the archipelago's essence without rushing.

10-Day Island-Hopping Adventure

For the adventurous traveller eager to dive deep into the diversity of the Dodecanese, this itinerary combines well-known gems with hidden treasures. It's paced to allow ample time on each island to soak in local life, venture off the beaten path, and indulge in activities from hiking to water sports.

Day 1-3: Rhodes – History, Beaches & Nightlife

- Spend the first three days as in the 5-day itinerary but include extra experiences such as a day trip to the Valley of the Butterflies and a visit to the Acropolis of Kamiros for hiking and archaeological exploration.
- Try water sports at Elli Beach, and explore local markets for unique crafts.

Day 4-5: Symi – Glamour and Charm

- Ferry to Symi (approx. 1 hour). Explore the vibrant harbor with its pastel neoclassical buildings.
- Visit the Panormitis Monastery and enjoy boat trips to secluded coves.
- Discover traditional sponge diving heritage and savour seafood fresh from the harbor.
- Hike to the castle ruins for panoramic views.

Day 6-7: Kalymnos – Adventure and Tradition

- Ferry to Kalymnos (approx. 1 hour). Known globally for rock climbing, spend a day learning or practicing on world-class limestone cliffs.
- Visit sponge diving museums to understand the island's maritime heritage.
- Explore local villages like Vathys and enjoy homemade dishes.
- Relax on serene beaches such as Myrties or Massouri.

Day 8: Karpathos – Untamed Nature & Villages

- Fly or ferry to Karpathos (flight recommended for time-saving).
- Spend your day hiking the rugged trails near Olympos village, an untouched settlement preserving traditional customs and dress.
- Swim in pristine coves and try local goat cheese and honey.

Day 9: Leros – History & Tranquillity

- Ferry to Leros. Explore the WWII military sites and the Castle of Panteli.
- Wander through the picturesque town of Agia Marina.
- Enjoy quiet beaches such as Alinda or Xerokambos.

Day 10: Return to Rhodes & Farewell

- Ferry or flight back to Rhodes.
- Use your last day for shopping, revisiting favourite spots, or simply relaxing before departure.

Why this itinerary works for adventurers:

It offers a balanced blend of active pursuits (climbing, hiking, exploring ancient ruins) and cultural immersion. The island-hopping sequence minimizes travel time while maximizing discovery, with diverse landscapes and authentic experiences.

Practical Tips for Both Itineraries

- Inter-island ferries: Book tickets in advance during peak season. Some smaller routes may run less frequently.
- Accommodations: Reserve lodgings early, especially on smaller islands.
- Local transport: Renting a scooter or car can increase flexibility on islands like Rhodes and Kos.
- Packing: Prepare for both beachwear and hiking gear.
- Cultural respect: Be mindful of local customs, especially when visiting religious sites.
- Hydration and sun protection: Essential year-round in the Aegean climate.

These tailored itineraries provide a clear roadmap for exploring the Dodecanese, each designed to match different travel styles and timeframes. By following these carefully curated plans, you'll avoid common pitfalls like rushed sightseeing or missed highlights, ensuring a rich, immersive, and unforgettable Greek island experience.

2-Week Explorer's Journey (Mix of Culture, Nature & Relaxation)

For travelers with ample time and an insatiable curiosity, this 14-day journey offers a deep dive into the diverse worlds of the Dodecanese islands. It blends the must-see cultural landmarks with lesser-known natural wonders, interspersed with moments of pure relaxation. The pace is moderate, allowing you to savour each experience fully while exploring a range of island atmospheres—from bustling harbors to tranquil villages.

Days 1-4: Rhodes – A Grand Introduction

- Begin your adventure in Rhodes, where history and modernity dance seamlessly.
- Spend a full day exploring the Medieval Old Town in detail—don't rush the Palace of the Grand Master or the Archaeological Museum.
- Venture beyond town to the Valley of the Butterflies for a nature walk, or visit the ancient ruins of Kamiros.
- Dedicate a day to beach time at Tsambika or Ladiko, perfect for swimming or water sports.
- Sample fine dining at a rooftop restaurant overlooking the city's illuminated walls.

Days 5-6: Symi – Picturesque Charm & Maritime Heritage

- Ferry to Symi, an island that feels like a postcard come to life with its pastel houses and vibrant harbor.
- Visit the Panormitis Monastery, a spiritual and architectural jewel nestled at the southern tip.
- Explore hidden coves by boat, or hike the trails above the harbor for sweeping views.

- Dive into local culinary delights featuring freshly caught seafood and island herbs.

Days 7-8: Kalymnos – Adventure & Tradition

- Head to Kalymnos, famed as a rock climbing mecca and for its sponge diving history.
- Take a guided climbing course or explore beginner routes for a thrilling adrenaline fix.
- Visit the Sponge Diving Museum and the quaint village of Vathy, savoring traditional dishes like *kapamas* (slow-cooked meat stew).
- Relax on quiet beaches such as Myrties, basking in the Aegean sun.

Days 9-10: Karpathos – Untamed Nature & Culture

- Fly or ferry to Karpathos for raw natural beauty and authentic village life.
- Trek from Olympos village, where women still wear traditional costumes and customs thrive.
- Discover pristine beaches like Apella and Kyra Panagia, perfect for swimming and snorkelling.
- Experience local music and dance at village festivals if timing aligns.

Days 11-12: Patmos – Spiritual Depth & Tranquillity

- Journey to Patmos, known as the "Jerusalem of the Aegean" for its religious significance.
- Explore the Monastery of Saint John and the Cave of the Apocalypse, tracing early Christian history.
- Spend quiet afternoons at secluded beaches like Meloi or Psili Ammos, absorbing the island's calm.
- Sample homemade sweets such as *baklava* paired with local honey.

Days 13-14: Leros & Lipsi – Peace & Off-the-Beaten-Path Beauty

- Ferry to Leros for a blend of WWII history and peaceful coastal villages.
- Walk the Castle of Panteli and explore charming harbors like Agia Marina.
- For your final day, take a short ferry to Lipsi, a tiny island with crystal-clear waters, traditional tavernas, and blissful tranquillity.
- End your trip with a sunset dinner overlooking the Aegean, reflecting on two weeks of unforgettable discovery.

Why this itinerary works for explorers:

This journey balances intense cultural immersion with leisurely days, appealing to travelers eager to experience the full spectrum of the Dodecanese. The mixture of historical sites, outdoor adventure, and quiet beaches creates a rhythm that satisfies body, mind, and spirit.

Honeymoon & Romantic Escape

The Dodecanese offers an idyllic setting for couples seeking romance, intimacy, and unforgettable memories. This carefully crafted itinerary focuses on enchanting landscapes, intimate dining, and serene moments that make the perfect honeymoon or romantic getaway.

Days 1-3: Rhodes – Historic Romance & Sunset Views

- Begin in Rhodes Old Town, strolling hand-in-hand through lantern-lit medieval streets.

- Book a romantic suite in a boutique hotel within the Old Town walls or a luxurious resort by the sea.
- Enjoy a private dinner on a rooftop terrace overlooking the city or the shimmering sea.
- Take a sunset cruise along the coastline, with local wine and meze to toast your new beginning.

Days 4-6: Symi – Picturesque Harbor & Cozy Corners

- Ferry to Symi, a jewel of pastel-hued buildings and narrow cobblestone lanes perfect for slow, romantic exploration.
- Stay in a charming boutique guesthouse with sea views.
- Explore the island's stunning coves by private boat or kayak, stopping for a secluded swim.
- Share intimate meals of freshly grilled octopus and local cheeses at quiet seaside tavernas.

Days 7-8: Astypalaia – Cycladic Charm Meets Dodecanese Serenity

- Fly or ferry to Astypalaia, known for its dramatic whitewashed architecture and butterfly-shaped coastline.
- Book a cave house or villa carved into the hillside, offering privacy and spectacular sunsets.
- Wander the castle-topped Chora village, with its winding streets perfect for romantic walks.
- Relax on the beaches of Livadi or Kaminakia, enjoying a picnic of local olives, bread, and wine.

Days 9-10: Patmos – Spiritual Tranquillity & Quiet Beaches

- Head to Patmos, a place of calm and reflection, perfect for couples seeking peace.
- Visit the Monastery of Saint John and spend time at the Cave of the Apocalypse.
- Take quiet beach walks along Meloi or Grikos.

- Arrange a private dinner at a cliffside restaurant overlooking the Aegean.

Days 11-12: Halki – Off-the-Grid Bliss

- Ferry to Halki, a tiny island that's intimate, quiet, and filled with charm.
- Stay in a restored neoclassical home, enjoying privacy and personalized service.
- Spend days swimming in crystal-clear waters, exploring peaceful harbors, and cycling through olive groves.
- Dine on fresh seafood under the stars, the only sounds being gentle waves.

Days 13-14: Relaxation & Farewell on Rhodes or Kos

- Return to Rhodes or Kos for a final night of pampering at a spa resort or beachside hotel.
- Enjoy a couples' massage, gourmet dining, and a last sunset stroll along the shore.
- Reflect on your romantic journey through the Dodecanese as you prepare for your departure.

Why this itinerary works for couples:

It offers the perfect balance of historic ambiance, natural beauty, and intimate experiences, with just enough activity to keep days interesting but never rushed. The handpicked accommodations and romantic dining options ensure your trip feels special from start to finish.

When planning your journey, consider these additional tips for the best experience:

- Book accommodations and ferries well in advance, especially during the high season.

- Customize each day according to your energy and mood; the Dodecanese's relaxed pace encourages spontaneity.
- Take advantage of local guides for deeper insights, especially in historic and natural sites.
- Pack layers and versatile gear to accommodate beach days and cooler evenings.
- Stay open to unexpected discoveries — some of the most memorable moments come from wandering off the planned path.

Family-Friendly Dodecanese Itinerary

Traveling with kids or multi-generational family members requires a special balance of fun, safety, and cultural enrichment. This itinerary is thoughtfully designed to keep every member — from toddlers to grandparents — engaged and comfortable, blending hands-on activities, gentle exploration, and downtime for rest and play. The Dodecanese offers an excellent mix of sandy beaches, historical wonders, and friendly locals, making it an ideal destination for families seeking a memorable yet stress-free vacation.

Days 1-3: Rhodes – History Meets Play

- Begin in Rhodes with visits to the Medieval Old Town, where kids can imagine knights and castles as they explore the Palace of the Grand Master and the fortified walls. Interactive guided tours or treasure hunt-style excursions bring history to life for younger travelers.
- Spend an afternoon at the Aquarium of Rhodes, perfect for little marine enthusiasts.
- Enjoy beach days at Elli Beach, where calm waters and nearby playgrounds make it easy for parents to relax while kids swim or build sandcastles.

- Dine at family-friendly tavernas with kid-approved menus and shaded outdoor seating.

Days 4-5: Kos – Playful Beaches & Nature Trails

- Ferry to Kos, an island with excellent family-oriented beaches like Tigaki and Mastichari featuring shallow waters and soft sand.
- Visit the Kos Natural Park or the interactive Archeological Museum, which offers engaging exhibits for all ages.
- Rent bicycles with child seats or explore the island on foot through easy trails.
- Enjoy meals at casual seaside eateries offering fresh grilled fish, Greek salads, and classic desserts like *loukoumades* (Greek doughnuts).

Days 6-8: Kalymnos – Adventure with Safety

- Head to Kalymnos, known for its outdoor activities. Families can enjoy gentle rock climbing courses designed for beginners and children, under expert supervision.
- Visit the Sponge Diving Museum, where kids learn about this unique local tradition through hands-on displays.
- Spend relaxed afternoons on beaches like Myrties, where calm waters and natural shade make it comfortable for young children.
- Opt for family villas or apartments with kitchen facilities, providing flexibility for meal times and snacks.

Days 9-10: Patmos – Culture & Calm

- Ferry to Patmos for a slower pace. Visit the Monastery of Saint John, and encourage older kids to learn stories behind the Cave of the Apocalypse through illustrated guides or audio tours.

- Spend time on shallow, sandy beaches such as Psili Ammos, where families can snorkel and spot colorful fish in safe waters.
- Choose accommodations with family suites or interconnected rooms, plus amenities like pools or playgrounds.

Days 11-12: Leros or Kos – Relax & Reflect

- Return to Leros or Kos for two days of relaxation at family-friendly resorts with pools, kid's clubs, and organized activities.
- Explore local markets where children can try fresh fruits and traditional sweets, or participate in craft workshops.
- End the trip with a sunset walk on the beach and a farewell dinner at a taverna with live music suitable for all ages.

Why this itinerary works for families:

It balances sightseeing with child-friendly activities and plenty of downtime, ensuring that no one feels overwhelmed. Safety, convenience, and opportunities for learning and play are woven throughout, creating an enriching experience for travelers of all ages.

Solo Traveller's Self-Discovery Path

For the solo traveller seeking transformation, reflection, and authentic connections, the Dodecanese offers an inspiring backdrop. This itinerary encourages mindful exploration, cultural immersion, and personal growth through a mix of solo-friendly activities, tranquil spots, and social hubs where new friendships can blossom.

Days 1-3: Rhodes – Dive Into History & Social Scenes

- Begin your journey in Rhodes, exploring the Medieval Old Town on your own terms—get lost in alleyways, visit the museums, and soak up the atmosphere at bustling cafes and markets.
- Join a walking tour tailored for solo travelers or a cooking class to learn Greek recipes and meet like-minded explorers.
- Spend evenings at lively squares like Eleftherias, perfect for solo dining or casual chats with locals and fellow travelers.
- Take time for personal reflection with a sunset stroll along Elli Beach.

Days 4-6: Nisyros – Spiritual & Natural Retreat

- Ferry to Nisyros, a quiet volcanic island ideal for introspection and nature hikes.
- Visit the Stefanos Crater for a surreal experience walking along active volcanic landscapes, a metaphorical journey of transformation.
- Stay in a small guesthouse or monastery guesthouse for a peaceful atmosphere and local insights.
- Attend local cultural events or festivals if available, to mingle and experience authentic island life.

Days 7-9: Patmos – Spirituality & Solitude

- Patmos invites solo travelers to delve deeper into spiritual and historical discovery.
- Participate in meditation sessions or quiet walks around the Monastery of Saint John and the Cave of the Apocalypse.
- Enjoy time at secluded beaches like Meloi for swimming and journaling or sketching.
- Join small group excursions, offering balance between solitude and social interaction.

Days 10-12: Karpathos – Wilderness & Community

- Visit Karpathos to challenge yourself with hiking untamed trails and discovering traditional villages like Olympos.
- Stay with local families or in small pensions to experience island hospitality firsthand.
- Engage in workshops such as traditional music or crafts, fostering meaningful cultural exchange.
- Allow yourself to disconnect fully in nature, finding quietude on pristine beaches.

Days 13-14: Kos – Wellness & Reflection

- Conclude in Kos, where wellness centers offer yoga classes, spa treatments, and detox programs.
- Spend your last days indulging in healthy local cuisine and gentle beach walks.
- Reflect on your journey with a journal or photography, capturing the essence of your solo adventure.
- Connect with new friends over farewell dinners or casual coffee meet-ups.

Why this itinerary works for solo travelers:

It balances solitude with opportunities to engage socially, providing enriching experiences that nurture self-discovery, cultural understanding, and personal well-being.

Eco-Conscious & Off-the-Grid Retreats

The Dodecanese is emerging as a prime destination for travelers seeking sustainable, environmentally conscious experiences. This itinerary is designed for eco-travelers who prioritize low-impact travel, respect for local ecosystems, and authentic off-the-beaten-path encounters. It includes eco-lodges, organic farm visits, conservation projects, and quiet natural havens.

Days 1-3: Tilos – Pioneer in Sustainability

- Start in Tilos, a UNESCO-recognized "European Island of Sustainability."
- Stay in eco-friendly accommodations powered by renewable energy, such as solar-heated guesthouses or eco-resorts.
- Join guided nature walks focused on the island's reforestation and conservation efforts protecting endangered species like the Mediterranean monk seal.
- Volunteer for half-day conservation activities or participate in beach clean-ups.

Days 4-6: Leros & Lipsi – Quiet Villages & Sustainable Farming

- Ferry to Leros or Lipsi, islands embracing traditional agricultural methods and slow tourism.
- Visit organic farms growing olives, herbs, and vegetables; participate in harvesting or cooking workshops.
- Explore untouched beaches and marine protected areas by kayak or on foot to minimize environmental impact.
- Choose accommodations that prioritize waste reduction and locally sourced materials.

Days 7-9: Astypalaia – Electric Island & Authentic Culture

- Astypalaia is gaining attention for its electric vehicle fleet and renewable energy projects.
- Rent an electric scooter or bicycle to explore the island quietly and cleanly.
- Stay in small family-run guesthouses committed to sustainable tourism practices.
- Attend workshops on local crafts using natural materials, supporting traditional artisans.

Days 10-12: Symi – Marine Conservation & Cultural Respect

- Visit Symi with a focus on its marine environment, home to diverse species and sponge diving heritage.
- Take part in responsible snorkelling tours that educate on reef preservation.
- Support local businesses emphasizing zero waste, such as cafes serving organic food in compostable packaging.
- Explore historical sites while practicing Leave No Trace principles.

Days 13-14: Rhodes – Closing with Green Luxury

- Return to Rhodes to experience eco-conscious luxury at hotels with sustainable certifications.
- Indulge in farm-to-table dining and spa treatments using natural, local products.
- Reflect on your eco-journey with a final hike in the island's protected natural parks.
- Use public transport or electric shuttles to navigate, minimizing your carbon footprint.

Why this itinerary works for eco-conscious travelers:

It provides immersive, hands-on experiences that contribute positively to island communities and ecosystems. Every choice supports sustainability, making your vacation both memorable and responsible.

CHAPTER

8

Practical Resources & Final Insights

SIM Cards, Wi-Fi & Staying Connected

When you step off the plane or ferry into the sun-drenched islands of the Dodecanese, one of the first questions you might have—beyond where to grab a souvlaki—is how to stay connected. Whether you're a digital nomad needing steady Wi-Fi for work, a family coordinating meetups, or an explorer sharing breath-taking sunsets on Instagram, understanding your connectivity options is crucial.

Local SIM Cards: Your Best Bet for Flexibility and Coverage
In the Dodecanese, Greek mobile networks provide robust coverage on the main islands—Rhodes, Kos, Patmos—but signal strength can fluctuate on smaller, remote islets like Arki or Kasos. For most travelers, purchasing a local SIM card upon arrival is the most economical and practical way to maintain seamless connectivity.

Major Greek telecom providers include Cosmote, Vodafone Greece, and Wind Hellas. Cosmote is generally recognized as the leader in both coverage and speed across the islands. You can buy prepaid SIM cards at airports (Rhodes and Kos have convenient kiosks), local mobile shops, or even some supermarkets. The process is straightforward: present your passport, choose a data package, and the staff will help activate the SIM immediately.

Data Packages: Depending on your needs, packages range from as little as 5GB for casual browsing and map use, to unlimited data plans perfect for streaming, video calls, and remote work. Prices vary but expect around €10-20 for a solid 10GB plan lasting 30 days. If you plan on island hopping, make sure your SIM allows roaming within Greece, which most do.

Wi-Fi Availability: Where to Expect It and Where You Don't
Most hotels, guesthouses, and cafés in the Dodecanese offer free Wi-Fi, but speeds and reliability vary widely. Urban centers like Rhodes Old Town and Kos Town generally provide strong

connections, ideal for video calls or uploading travel photos. In smaller villages or eco-lodges, Wi-Fi can be spotty or intentionally limited to encourage digital detox.

If you rely heavily on Wi-Fi, consider these tips:

- Carry a portable Wi-Fi hotspot device (MiFi): You can rent or buy these at major airports or electronics stores. It's a reliable backup, especially if you're moving frequently.
- Download offline maps and guides: Google Maps and apps like Maps.me allow offline navigation, essential for hiking or wandering islands with poor signal.
- Use apps for connectivity: WhatsApp, Viber, and Messenger are popular communication tools in Greece and work well on data or Wi-Fi. Many local businesses also use these apps to communicate with customers.

Staying Connected Without Breaking the Bank: To avoid unexpected roaming charges, switch your phone to airplane mode and use Wi-Fi or your Greek SIM exclusively while traveling. If you're staying for a longer time or working remotely, local providers sometimes offer special rates for extended stays—ask about these at the point of purchase.

Public Transport, Driving & Local Navigation Tips

The Dodecanese archipelago's charm lies partly in its accessibility: whether you want to explore bustling town centers, hidden beaches, or rugged mountain trails, getting around efficiently will define your experience. However, navigating the islands' transport systems and roads requires some insider knowledge to maximize your time and safety.

Public Transport: Buses and Ferries

Each major island has a reliable public bus network connecting key towns, beaches, and archaeological sites, but frequencies can vary, especially outside the peak summer months. Rhodes and Kos have the best bus infrastructure, making it easy for visitors without cars to explore.

- **Rhodes**: The KTEL bus system covers the airport, city, beaches, and smaller villages. Tickets are affordable— usually under €3 per ride. Bus schedules are posted online and at stations, but always double-check for seasonal changes.
- **Kos**: Similar to Rhodes, buses serve the main town, beaches, and airport. Bus drivers are helpful, but routes may be confusing if you're unfamiliar with local names, so keep your destination written in Greek or use a map app.
- **Smaller Islands:** Patmos, Symi, and others operate more limited bus services, sometimes only a few runs daily. Check schedules in advance and consider taxis or rental vehicles for flexible travel.

Ferries:
Inter-island ferries are the lifeblood of the Dodecanese and come in a range of types, from slow car ferries to speedy catamarans. Booking tickets online in advance is advisable during peak season. Ferry ports are well-signposted, but arriving early is key as lines can get long.

Driving: The Best Way to Explore Off-the-Beaten-Path

For freedom and adventure, renting a car, scooter, or ATV is the way to go, especially on larger islands like Rhodes, Kos, Karpathos, or Kalymnos. Roads vary from modern highways to narrow, winding mountain paths — an exhilarating experience for confident drivers but potentially challenging for the inexperienced.

Driver's License and Requirements:

Most rental agencies require an international driving permitalongside your national license if it's not in Latin characters. Greek traffic laws are generally similar to the rest of Europe, but expect relaxed enforcement in rural areas.

Road Conditions and Tips:

- Main roads on Rhodes and Kos are well maintained, with clear signage.
- Secondary roads on smaller islands can be narrow and steep, often without guardrails—drive cautiously, especially at night.
- Watch out for wandering livestock, especially on Karpathos and Astypalaia.
- In villages, be mindful of pedestrians, scooters, and occasional donkeys crossing the road.
- Parking in popular spots can be tight during summer—arrive early or park in designated lots to avoid fines.

Scooters and ATVs:

For single travelers or couples, renting a scooter or ATV offers an eco-friendly, fun way to explore. Helmets are mandatory and always wear protective gear. Remember that weather conditions like sudden summer storms can impact safety.

Taxis and Ride-Sharing:

Taxis are available but limited outside main towns and peak hours. It's best to book rides via hotel reception or apps where available. Unlike big cities, ride-sharing apps like Uber or Lyft are not widely used here, so traditional taxis and car rentals remain primary options.

Local Navigation Tips:

- Use Google Maps or Maps.me for driving and walking directions, but have a physical map as backup for remote areas with spotty reception.
- Ask locals for directions if unsure — Greeks are famously hospitable and often happy to help with detailed advice.
- Keep your destination names handy in Greek script to show drivers or locals.
- Be flexible with your itinerary; unexpected detours often lead to the most memorable discoveries.

Connecting to the digital world while embracing the unplugged beauty of the islands is a balancing act every traveller faces here. By equipping yourself with a local SIM card or portable hotspot, you ensure reliable communication without frustration. Meanwhile, understanding public transport nuances and local driving realities lets you maximize your island adventures safely and comfortably.

Embrace the slower rhythms of the Dodecanese but remain informed and prepared, and you'll navigate these sun-kissed islands with confidence and ease, turning every trip moment into a seamless blend of discovery and relaxation.

Accessibility Info for Travelers with Disabilities

Traveling to the Dodecanese for those with disabilities or mobility challenges requires careful planning, but it's far from impossible. Over recent years, awareness and infrastructure improvements have steadily increased across the islands, though conditions vary widely depending on location and type of disability. This section offers an honest, detailed look at accessibility and practical tips to ensure all travelers enjoy a rewarding visit.

The Dodecanese's mix of ancient architecture, narrow cobblestone streets, and rugged landscapes pose challenges for accessibility. Major towns like Rhodes and Kos have made significant strides in creating wheelchair-friendly paths, ramps, and accessible beaches. However, many smaller or remote islands, especially those with steep terrain like Karpathos and Astypalaia, remain difficult for travelers with mobility limitations.

Island-by-Island Accessibility Highlights:

- **Rhodes**: Rhodes Town's medieval Old Town is partially accessible; some historic sites offer ramps and lifts, but many narrow alleys remain challenging. The newer parts of town and resort areas have more accessible hotels and facilities. Beaches like Elli Beach have dedicated accessibility features such as ramps and special beach wheelchairs.
- **Kos**: The main town is quite accessible, with flat promenades and accessible buses available. Some public beaches provide ramps and accessible toilets. The Asklepion archaeological site has partial wheelchair access but uneven terrain.
- **Patmos and Symi**: Accessibility is limited. Both islands have many stairs and steep hills, making wheelchair travel difficult. Some accommodations offer ground-floor rooms, but public infrastructure is minimal.
- **Kalymnos & Karpathos**: The rugged terrain limits accessibility; however, select hotels cater to special needs travelers. Assistance may be necessary for excursions.
- **Smaller Islands (Lipsi, Agathonisi, Arki)**: Minimal facilities exist, making these better suited to travelers with full mobility.

Accommodations and Facilities:

When booking, request information on specific accessibility features, such as step-free entrances, adapted bathrooms, elevators, and proximity to public transport or beaches. Many hotels on Rhodes and Kos advertise accessibility; boutique stays and family-run guesthouses may be more variable.

Transportation:

- **Buses**: On Rhodes and Kos, some buses are wheelchair accessible, but availability can be limited. Always confirm in advance and arrive early to secure a spot.
- **Taxis**: Accessible taxis are rare but may be booked through local services in major towns.
- **Ferries**: Large ferries usually offer wheelchair access with ramps and adapted restrooms, but smaller boats may not. Confirm with ferry companies before travel.

Beaches:

Accessible beaches tend to be in more developed areas, with features like wooden pathways, accessible sunbeds, and special beach wheelchairs (available for free at some beaches). Elli Beach in Rhodes and Psalidi Beach in Kos are among the most well-equipped.

Practical Tips for Travelers with Disabilities:

- Inform your accommodation, ferry, and transport providers well in advance about your requirements.
- Bring any necessary mobility aids and a lightweight travel wheelchair if possible.
- Use local support services or travel companions when visiting rugged or historical sites.
- Contact local tourism offices on Rhodes and Kos for the most updated accessibility info.

- Consider medical travel insurance that covers specialized equipment and emergency evacuation.

Useful Apps & Travel Numbers

The digital age makes exploring the Dodecanese easier than ever, with a range of websites, apps, and essential contacts designed to keep you informed, safe, and entertained. Bookmark or download these before you travel to streamline your experience.

Accommodation Booking Platforms:

- Booking.com, Airbnb, and Vrbo are popular for finding everything from hotels to villas. Use filters to identify family-friendly, accessible, or boutique options.

Travel Apps to Download:

- Google Maps / Maps.me: Essential for offline navigation and discovering hidden spots.
- XE Currency: Real-time currency converter to manage your budget effectively.
- Google Translate: Helpful for translating signs, menus, or basic conversations.
- WhatsApp / Viber: Widely used for communication locally and internationally.
- Weather Apps: Accuweather or Windy to stay updated on island weather, especially important for ferry or sailing plans.

Emergency Numbers (Greece-wide):

- 112: European-wide emergency number for police, ambulance, and fire services.
- 100: Police emergency.

- 166: Ambulance services.
- 199: Fire department.
- Tourist Police (Rhodes and Kos): Provides assistance for travelers in need. Contact details vary by island—ask your hotel or local tourism office for specifics.

Health and Safety Resources:

- Nearest Hospitals: Rhodes General Hospital, Kos General Hospital, and local clinics on other islands.
- Pharmacies: Open during business hours, with emergency pharmacies available at night—ask locals or hotel staff.

Local Customs & Communication:

- Keep printed copies of important phone numbers, your hotel's contact info, and embassy details.
- Many locals speak basic English, but learning a few Greek phrases (see Language Guide in this book) enhances your experience.

Traveling through the Dodecanese offers a beautiful blend of ancient history, crystal-clear waters, and vibrant island life. By preparing ahead with the right connectivity tools, accessibility knowledge, and trusted local resources, you'll unlock the islands' full magic without unnecessary stress. Whether you're seeking adventure, relaxation, cultural immersion, or a bit of all three, the practical insights here are designed to empower you to travel smarter and enjoy every moment of your 2025 Dodecanese journey.

Island Emergency Services Directory

When exploring the Dodecanese, safety and preparedness are paramount. Having a clear, organized directory of emergency services across the islands can be a literal lifesaver. The diversity of islands, varying infrastructure, and sometimes remote locations mean travelers should keep essential contacts handy.

General Emergency Number:

- 112 — This is the pan-European emergency number, connecting you instantly to local police, fire, or medical assistance anywhere in Greece.

Rhodes Emergency Contacts:

- Police: +30 22410 26242 (Rhodes Police Headquarters)
- Tourist Police: +30 22410 23421 — Dedicated to assisting tourists with security, lost items, or legal concerns.
- Fire Department: +30 22410 27222
- Hospital: Rhodes General Hospital, +30 22410 25400 — Equipped for emergencies, with an emergency room and ambulance services.
- Ambulance: 166 or through hospital direct.
- Coast Guard: +30 22410 28700 — Vital for sea emergencies, lost swimmers, or boat incidents.

Kos Emergency Contacts:

- Police: +30 22420 29100
- Tourist Police: +30 22420 24506
- Fire Department: +30 22420 22222
- Hospital: Kos General Hospital, +30 22420 28400 — Provides emergency care and ambulance.
- Ambulance: 166

- Coast Guard: +30 22420 26300

Patmos Emergency Contacts:

- Police: +30 22470 31300
- Fire Department: +30 22470 31306
- Health Center: +30 22470 31314
- Ambulance: 166
- Coast Guard: +30 22470 31221

Other Islands:

Many smaller islands have local police stations, health centers, and volunteer fire departments but may lack full hospital facilities. In emergencies, medical evacuation to Rhodes or Kos is often necessary. Below are some key numbers:

- Kalymnos Police: +30 22430 22222
- Karpathos Police: +30 22450 21300
- Leros Police: +30 22470 22451
- Nisyros Health Center: +30 22470 31210
- Astypalaia Police: +30 22470 31230
- Kos Coast Guard: +30 22420 26300 (for inter-island emergencies)

Tips for Using Emergency Services:

- Always carry your passport or ID and insurance info.
- Use the 112 number if unsure which service to call; operators can dispatch the right help.
- Inform your accommodation of any health concerns or special needs.
- In case of sea emergencies, contact the Coast Guard immediately.
- Learn basic Greek emergency phrases like "Βοήθεια!" (Help!) and "Έχω έκτακτη ανάγκη" (I have an emergency).

Final Advice: Avoiding Tourist Traps & Making It Meaningful

The Dodecanese Islands beckon with authentic charm, historical riches, and crystalline seas, but like any popular destination, they come with their share of tourist traps. Avoiding these pitfalls can transform your trip from a routine checklist to a genuinely enriching experience.

Recognizing Tourist Traps:

Tourist traps often manifest as overpriced eateries with mediocre food, souvenir shops with mass-produced goods, or overly crowded beaches and attractions lacking authenticity. These spots usually cater to high-volume, low-quality visits and do little to deepen your understanding or appreciation of the islands.

- **Overpriced Dining:** Beware restaurants in the busiest harbors or near main tourist hubs charging premium prices for average meals. Genuine island cuisine thrives in family-run tavernas tucked away from the main streets.
- **Generic Souvenirs:** Markets selling plastic trinkets and low-quality products offer little connection to the local culture. Seek artisan markets, local craftspeople, and authentic handmade goods.
- **Crowded Beaches**: Some beaches attract day-trippers in droves, leaving little space and a diluted experience. Venture to less accessible coves or islands for tranquillity.

Tips to Avoid Tourist Traps:

1. **Do Your Homework:** Use trusted local guides, updated travel forums, and reviews from verified travelers. This guide itself is designed to point you toward genuine experiences.

2. **Venture Off the Beaten Path:** Explore lesser-known islands, inland villages, and remote hiking trails. These offer deeper cultural immersion and fewer crowds.
3. **Engage with Locals:** Strike up conversations in tavernas, markets, or shops. Locals often share hidden gems unavailable to the average tourist.
4. **Choose Quality Over Quantity:** Opt for fewer activities done well rather than packing your itinerary with superficial stops.
5. **Respect Local Culture:** Observe customs, dress codes, and etiquette to gain respect and open doors to authentic experiences.
6. **Support Sustainable Tourism:** Patronize businesses that prioritize local produce, environmental care, and community involvement.

Making It Meaningful: How to Truly Connect with the Dodecanese

- **Attend a Village Festival:** These colorful, vibrant celebrations offer insight into island traditions, music, dance, and food. Whether it's the feast of a local saint or a harvest celebration, participation is unforgettable.
- **Try Hands-On Experiences:** Take a cooking class, join a sponge diving trip, or learn traditional weaving. These activities deepen appreciation beyond sightseeing.
- **Explore History with Context:** Visit archaeological sites with a knowledgeable guide or use an audio tour app. Stories behind ruins and castles bring the past alive.
- **Spend Time with Islanders:** Slow down your pace and share coffee or ouzo with locals. These moments often become travel highlights.
- **Practice Responsible Tourism:** Leave no trace, avoid disturbing wildlife, and respect local customs to ensure the islands remain beautiful for future visitors.

The magic of the Dodecanese lies in its balance of ancient and modern, wild nature and welcoming towns, adventure and relaxation. Avoiding tourist traps and immersing yourself fully will ensure you don't just visit these islands—you connect with them. Your journey becomes part of their living story and yours to cherish forever.

CHAPTER

9

Conclusion

A s you prepare to explore the enchanting Dodecanese, the key to a truly unforgettable journey lies not just in visiting the islands but in connecting deeply with their unique spirit. This guide has equipped you with practical tools, insightful itineraries, and local knowledge to help you navigate everything from bustling harbors to tranquil, hidden gems. But beyond the logistics and sightseeing, the heart of your trip will be shaped by how you engage—with the culture, the people, and the landscape.

Avoiding tourist traps is essential to preserving the authenticity and joy of your experience. Instead of chasing crowds and generic souvenirs, seek out the quiet corners where tradition thrives and hospitality is genuine. Slow down, listen to local stories, savour handmade cuisine, and embrace the rhythms of island life. These moments transform a standard holiday into a meaningful adventure that resonates long after you've left the shores.

Remember, the Dodecanese are more than just destinations—they are living communities rich with history, resilience, and warmth. Traveling responsibly, respecting customs, and supporting local businesses ensures these islands will remain vibrant and welcoming for generations to come.

Ultimately, the best travel experiences are those that leave you enriched and inspired. Whether you're a first-time visitor or a seasoned traveller, allow yourself to be curious and open, to venture beyond the obvious, and to create memories that go beyond the surface. This guide is your starting point; the true magic of the Dodecanese awaits in the discoveries you make along the way. Safe travels and joyful exploration!

Bonus Section

10 Island Quests – A Challenge for the Adventurous Soul

The Dodecanese archipelago is a treasure trove of unique landscapes, vibrant culture, and hidden wonders that reward those willing to step beyond the usual tourist trail. For travelers craving adventure, authenticity, and unforgettable stories, this section offers ten quests — challenges that will test your spirit, spark your curiosity, and deepen your connection to these islands. Each quest is a call to explore with intention and enthusiasm, blending natural wonders, history, and local culture into a truly immersive experience.

Can You Swim in a Volcanic Bay?

Nisyros, the volcanic island, invites you to plunge into warm, mineral-rich waters in the crater's caldera. Imagine floating in a natural hot spring surrounded by surreal lunar landscapes, where steam rises from fissures and sulphurous scents perfume the air. This unique swimming experience blends adventure with geology, offering not just a refreshing dip but a swim in the heart of an active volcano's legacy. Be sure to visit the famous Stefanos Crater, and after your swim, explore the charming villages dotted around the island.

Can You Climb the Walls of a Crusader Castle?

Rhodes, steeped in medieval grandeur, beckons the history buff and adventurer alike to scale the imposing walls of the Palace of the Grand Masters. Walk along battlements that once guarded knights and kings, where every stone tells stories of battles, sieges, and political intrigue. For the daring, climb the ramparts to capture breath-taking views over the Old Town's labyrinthine streets and the Aegean Sea beyond. This is a quest to experience history not as a distant observer but as an active participant in the island's past.

Can You Eat Like a Local in a Village No Tourists Know About?

On islands like Leros or Lipsi, wander off the beaten path and find family-run tavernas where menus aren't printed in multiple languages and dishes come from secret recipes passed down through generations. Here, your challenge is to immerse yourself in authentic island life: share a meal of freshly caught fish, wild greens, and homemade cheese while swapping stories with villagers. This quest isn't about convenience or trendiness; it's about connection and savoring flavors that have shaped the Dodecanese diet for centuries.

Can You Spot the Rare Monk Seal?

The Mediterranean monk seal is one of the world's rarest and most elusive marine mammals. Your quest is to seek out their protected habitats, especially around islands like Kalymnos and Halki. While sightings are rare and require patience and respect for wildlife, guided eco-tours increase your chances to witness these gentle creatures in their natural environment. This quest challenges you to embrace conservation-minded travel—appreciating nature's wonders without disturbing them.

Additional Quests to Complete Your Adventure:

– Can You Hike a Trail Less Travelled?

Explore the rugged paths of Karpathos or Tilos, where nature trails wind through wild landscapes, traditional villages, and panoramic views, far from tourist crowds. Challenge yourself to trek these routes, often marked by ancient shepherd paths and Byzantine chapels.

– Can You Sail to a Secret Beach?

Rent a boat or join a local skipper to discover hidden coves only accessible by sea. Whether on Symi or Astypalaia, these secluded beaches reward the patient explorer with crystal-clear waters and serene solitude.

– Can You Learn a Traditional Craft?

From sponge diving in Kalymnos to pottery in Kos, test your hands at a centuries-old trade. Workshops and local artisans welcome curious visitors eager to learn the skills that shaped island economies and culture.

– Can You Celebrate a Village Festival?

Time your visit to coincide with a local feast day or festival, such as the Feast of Panagia on Patmos or the Karpathos Cultural Festival. Participate in traditional dances, music, and communal meals—a joyous way to live the island spirit.

– Can You Navigate a Night Under the Stars?

Experience the islands after dark by camping in nature or taking a guided night hike. The Dodecanese's low light pollution offers spectacular stargazing, turning the night sky into a celestial map that connects travelers to ancient navigators.

Why Take the Island Quests?

These quests are more than just challenges; they're invitations to engage fully with the Dodecanese's soul. By stepping off the typical tourist routes, you gain access to richer stories, deeper connections, and memories that will last a lifetime. Each quest encourages curiosity, respect, and an adventurous spirit—qualities that transform ordinary travel into a meaningful journey.

So, are you ready to dive into volcanic waters, climb ancient walls, savour untouched flavors, and seek elusive wildlife? The islands are waiting, and these quests offer the perfect way to uncover their secrets. Embrace the challenge, and your Dodecanese adventure will be anything but ordinary.

Photo Challenge – 25 Shots to Capture the Soul of the Dodecanese

Photography isn't just about snapping pretty pictures — it's a way to connect, interpret, and preserve your journey. The Dodecanese offers a kaleidoscope of vibrant scenes, from the serene simplicity of whitewashed chapels to the bustling life of colorful harbors. This photo challenge invites you to slow down, observe deeply, and frame moments that reveal the soul of the islands.

Each shot on this curated list represents a story, a feeling, or a tradition unique to the Dodecanese. Whether you're wielding a professional camera or simply using your smartphone, this creative checklist will guide you to capture images that reflect both iconic sights and hidden gems, making your travel album a genuine narrative of your adventure.

1. Whitewashed Chapels Against Blue Skies

Tiny, pristine chapels dotting rocky hillsides or cliff edges are quintessentially Greek. Look for crisp white walls, cobalt doors, and fluttering prayer flags. Early morning or late afternoon light will add warmth and depth.

2. Vibrant Fishing Boats in Symi Harbor

Symi's harbor bursts with color—pastel-hued neoclassical houses mirror off the water, while traditional caiques bob gently. Capture the harmony of tradition and life on the sea.

3. Narrow Cobbled Streets in Rhodes Old Town

Frame the winding alleys lined with medieval stone walls, wrought-iron lanterns, and flower pots spilling over balconies. Look for candid shots of locals going about their day.

4. Sunset Over Lindos Acropolis, Rhodes

The golden hour casts a magical glow on the ancient ruins perched above the whitewashed village. A wide-angle shot capturing the contrast between sea, ruins, and village rooftops is a must.

5. Colorful Doors & Shutters in Kos Town

From faded turquoise to fiery red, doors and shutters reveal the island's Ottoman and Venetian past. Look for textured paint, peeling walls, and flower pots that add character.

6. The Volcanic Crater of Nisyros

Capture the surreal landscape of steaming vents, cracked earth, and vibrant mineral deposits in shades of orange, yellow, and grey. Early morning mists add mystery.

7. Sponge Divers at Work in Kalymnos

Document the centuries-old tradition of sponge diving—men hauling nets, preparing boats, and sorting sponges on sunlit docks.

8. Windmills Spinning on Astypalaia's Hills

Find a traditional windmill perched against the sky or overlooking azure waters. Capture the texture of the stone and the motion of the blades if the wind is strong.

9. Aegean Blue Waters in Hidden Coves

Seek out secluded beaches with crystal-clear turquoise waters framed by dramatic cliffs or pine forests. Shots from a kayak or drone can capture stunning perspectives.

10. Local Markets Bustling with Color and Life

Vivid displays of olives, spices, herbs, and handcrafted goods invite close-up shots bursting with texture and pattern.

11. Traditional Festivities & Folk Costumes

During festivals, photograph locals dressed in traditional costumes, dancing, or preparing feasts—authentic moments full of joy and heritage.

12. Ancient Ruins & Columns in Kos and Rhodes

Capture the weathered grandeur of ancient temples and mosaics, paying attention to the interplay of light and shadow.

13. Monastery Courtyards & Iconography

Focus on intricate religious icons, frescoes, and serene courtyards that reflect centuries of faith and artistry.

14. Café Life & Ouzo by the Waterfront

A candid moment of locals chatting over coffee or sipping ouzo by the sea, with reflections and light playing off glassware.

15. Lush Olive Groves & Vineyards

Rows of silver-green olive trees and terraced vineyards create patterns that tell of centuries of cultivation.

16. Colorful Bougainvillea Cascades

Bright magenta flowers spilling over stone walls or archways offer vibrant contrast to whitewashed buildings.

17. Rustic Village Life & Elderly Locals

Portraits of weathered faces, storytelling gestures, and traditional crafts in small villages like Leros or Kasos.

18. Dramatic Cliffs and Sea Caves

Capture the raw power of nature where sea meets rock, especially on Karpathos and Kalymnos, highlighting textures and movement.

19. Starry Night Skies Over Silent Islands

Long-exposure shots of the Milky Way over dark, quiet landscapes, perfect for astrophotographers.

20. Local Cuisine in Action

Close-ups of hands preparing fresh seafood, stacking pastries, or plating vibrant Greek salads.

21. Colorful Street Art & Murals

Surprising bursts of contemporary creativity blending with traditional architecture.

22. Traditional Fishing Nets Drying in the Sun

The intricate patterns and colors of nets strung between boats or on docks tell stories of a seafaring way of life.

23. Panoramic Views from Hilltop Villages

Sweeping shots capturing the patchwork of white buildings, olive groves, and endless sea beyond.

24. Quiet Beaches at Dawn

Empty sands and gentle waves bathed in soft morning light, evoking peaceful solitude.

25. Friendly Faces & Spontaneous Moments

Perhaps the most treasured shots—smiles, laughter, and interactions that reveal the warmth of the island communities.

How to Make the Most of This Challenge

Approach each shot with patience and respect—both for the environment and the people who live here. Use natural light whenever possible, and don't rush. Sometimes the best images come from waiting for the right moment or noticing small details others miss.

By completing this photo challenge, you're not only creating a stunning visual diary but also training your eye to see the Dodecanese through a lens of curiosity and appreciation. Share your favourite shots with friends or on social media, but always honour the islands' spirit by being a mindful traveller.

This challenge transforms photography into a journey of discovery—every frame a step closer to understanding the true soul of the Dodecanese.

Travel Journal Prompts & Reflection Pages

Travel is not just about places seen—it's about moments felt, connections made, and memories forged deep within. The Dodecanese Islands are a treasure trove of experiences that awaken all your senses, from the salty sea breeze to the warmth of local hospitality. To help you capture the true essence of your journey, this guide includes specially designed travel journal prompts and reflection pages, inviting you to slow down, reflect, and create your own story alongside this guide.

Whether you are a first-time visitor or a seasoned traveller, journaling transforms a trip into a rich, personal narrative that lasts far beyond the final sunset. These prompts encourage introspection and gratitude, helping you to connect more deeply with the islands and yourself. Writing about your experiences enhances your awareness and appreciation, turning fleeting moments into lasting treasures.

Capture Your Dodecanese Journey: Thoughtful Prompts to Inspire You

Write about the best sunrise you saw:

Was it the gentle glow over the Aegean Sea from a hidden beach on Karpathos? Or the fiery burst of colors illuminating Rhodes Old Town's medieval walls? Describe the colors, sounds, and feelings that washed over you. Did it change your perspective or set the tone for your day?

Describe the stranger who made your day:

Travel is as much about people as it is about places. Maybe a local shopkeeper shared a secret spot, or a fellow traveller became an unexpected companion. Write about their kindness, the conversation you shared, or the gesture that made your visit unforgettable.

Recall the food that made you cry happy tears:

Dodecanese cuisine is a feast for the senses and the soul. Was it a spoonful of sweet honey from a hillside apiary? Fresh octopus grilled to perfection on Symi? Or a rich spoonful of homemade baklava? Capture the taste, aroma, and emotion that food stirred inside you.

Describe a moment of unexpected beauty:

Perhaps a sudden rain shower created a rainbow over a quiet village, or you stumbled upon a deserted cove bathed in golden light. Reflect on these serendipitous discoveries that made your trip uniquely yours.

Write about your favourite local tradition or festival you witnessed: The vibrant celebrations across the islands offer glimpses into centuries-old culture. Was it the candlelit Easter procession in

Patmos, or a folk dance in a mountain village? Share what moved you about the experience.

Reflect on a challenge you overcame during your trip: Travel often brings surprises—missed ferries, language barriers, or unexpected detours. How did you handle these moments? What did they teach you about resilience and adventure?

Reflection Pages: Your Personal Dodecanese Story

Beyond the prompts, this guide includes dedicated reflection pages where you can freely write, sketch, or paste mementos like tickets and postcards. These blank or lined pages encourage spontaneous creativity, allowing you to chronicle daily highlights, thoughts, or even jot down new Greek words you've learned.

Taking time each day to reflect deepens your connection to the place and enriches your travel experience. These pages become a keepsake, a tangible memory book that you'll cherish long after your journey ends.

The Power of Reflection in Travel

Writing about your trip helps you pause and appreciate the richness of each moment, turning ordinary encounters into profound experiences. It trains you to observe more keenly, feel more deeply, and remember more vividly.

As you move through the islands—whether wandering the ancient streets of Rhodes, hiking in lush valleys on Tilos, or savoring sunset views in Astypalaia—let this journal be your companion. Use it to capture the laughter, the lessons, the quiet moments, and the exhilarating adventures.

By the end of your Dodecanese adventure, you will not just have visited these islands—you will have lived them, felt them, and carried them home within your heart and on these pages.

Printed in Dunstable, United Kingdom

67348020R00097